"Were beauty under twenty locks kept fast,
Yet love breaks through and picks them all at last."

WILLIAM SHAKESPEARE, *Venus and Adonis, I. 575.*

CONTENTS

Chapter   *Page*

  I. INTRODUCTION 1

  II. HISTORICAL SURVEY 10

  III. THE GIRDLE OF CHASTITY AND THE LAW 92

  IV. JOHN MOODIE, M.D. AND SURGEON 124

  V. THE GIRDLE OF CHASTITY IN LITERATURE 129

  VI. SUMMARY AND CONCLUDING REMARKS 160

     INDEX OF AUTHORITIES QUOTED 165

     INDEX OF SUBJECTS 168

LIST OF ILLUSTRATIONS

I. Design by Aldegrever . . . 48

II. Girdle of Chastity. Kyeser's " Bellifortis " (By permission of the Universitäts Bibliothek, Göttingen) . . . . . *To face p.* 49

III. Girdle of Chastity. Palazzo Ducale. Venice. (By permission of the Director) . . *To face p.* 64

IV. The jealous husband prepares for a journey. P. Fürst (?) (After E. Fuchs and A. Kind) *To face p.* 65

V. Girdle of Chastity. Museum. Kalmar *To face p.* 80

VI. Girdles of Chastity. Sammlung Erbach, Erbach, Odenwald *To face p.* 81

VII. Girdles of Chastity. Musée de Cluny, Paris. (By permission.) . . . . *To face p.* 96

VIII. Girdle of Chastity. Nordiska Museet, Stockholm. *To face p.* 97

PREFACE

THIS volume is an attempt to give the general and educated reader an account of one of the most curious results of jealousy ever invented by man. It would seem that in few directions is the fear of cuckoldom and the possibility of illegitimate offspring more vividly displayed than in the use of the so-called Girdle of Chastity.

My thanks are due to many friends who have given me advice and help. Among them I must mention the authorities and staffs of a number of great libraries of which the British Museum, the Bibliothèque Nationale, the Preussische Staatsbibliothek, the Library of Congress, the New York Public Library, the Library of the Surgeon-General's Office, Washington, D.C., and the Harvard College Library are the most important. Of individuals in these great institutions I must record my best thanks to Mr. A. Ellis, of the British Museum, and to Dr. Kurt Tautz, of the Preussische Staatsbibliothek, to both of whom I owe a special debt of gratitude for their help and advice.

PREFACE

I also wish to thank my friend Mr. B. W. Downs, of Christ's College, Cambridge, for much sage counsel and help in the translation of certain passages quoted herein; and also I have received assistance from my friend Mr. I. Gröndahl; from the Librarian of the Universitäts Bibliothek, Göttingen; from the Director of the Palazzo Ducale, Venice; from the authorities of the Sammlung Erbach, Erbach; and from other persons who have either photographed objects under their care or have given me information concerning them. To these, who have helped me in Paris, Stockholm, and elsewhere, I tender my best thanks, and also to Mr. Eduard Fuchs, who has permitted me to draw from the stores of his great histories, and also to my printers and publishers for the care they have bestowed on the preparation of the book.

In conclusion I must record the recognition and gratitude I owe to my wife, whose constant help and advice have been more valuable than can be adequately expressed.

E. J. DINGWALL.

CHAPTER I

INTRODUCTION

THE history of jealousy has, in the course of ages, provided many curious sidelights upon human nature, and poets and satirists have taken full advantage of this feature to enliven their themes. Even to-day the cuckold is often a subject for merriment although the gradual breakdown in traditional morality is robbing the cynic of one of the most fruitful sources of ribald jest and unholy mirth.

It is not easy for the modern reader to realize the extent and richness of the earlier literature of cuckoldom. The unfaithful wife and the deceived husband were the source of endless amusement in song and story, and the works of the French and Italian satirists and anti-feminists are full of droll incidents which go to prove the faithless character of women and the necessity of restraining them by cunning if not by force. Indeed, so difficult did it seem to prevent the married woman from indulging in illicit amours that the wildest expedients were discussed. The title of the German story, *Gegen der Weiber untreue helfen weder Riegel*

1

noch Schloss,[1] indicates an opinion which must have been widely held, although it would seem improbable that many spouses, distrustful of mere material restraints, determined upon the more drastic method so quaintly described by Poggio in one of his droll stories, where he tells the tale of a man, who, bent upon proving the infidelity of his wife, unmanned himself as a final and decisive test.[2]

Since the part played by jealousy in the domain of the sexual life is probably more important than in any other department of human activity, it is of interest to consider in detail certain of the queerer manifestations of this passion as they present themselves in fact and fancy, history and legend. Among these more bizarre aspects, the use of the so-called Girdle of Chastity is undoubtedly one of the most curious. The fundamental idea which lies behind and at the root of the chastity belt is exceedingly simple. Just as in the practice of male infibulation [3] the central idea is the prevention by force of the use of the generative organ, so in the use of the chastity belt is the external control of the *pudendum muliebre* the

---

[1] E. Fuchs, *Illustrierte Sittengeschichte vom Mittelalter bis zur Gegenwart* (6 vols., München, 1909–12), ii, pp. 150–1.

[2] B. Poggio, *Les facéties de Pogge* (2 vols., Paris, 1878), ccxxv, vol. ii, pp. 156–7 : cf. *Le Courrier facétieux* (Lyon, 1668), p. 317.

[3] E. J. Dingwall, *Male Infibulation* (London, 1925).

aim and object of the apparatus. In our former discussion of the mechanical methods which were in ancient times employed to ensure male continence we confined our attention to those which, rightly or wrongly, have been classed under the term " infibulation ". But we did not fail to observe that the term has had a far wider significance than that which we were then considering. We found that the term had also been applied to an operation upon the female, and that the custom of female infibulation was well known in many parts of the world. Now whatever may have been the original intention of female infibulation (and this volume does not concern itself with that problem) it is clear that certain forms of this practice can, and have, been employed as a means of preserving female continence. The infibulation of mares has long been known to the veterinary profession,[1] and there is no essential difference between it and the more primitive means of infibulating women. In principle the two are identical, and consist in fastening together the labia majora by means of a ring, fibula, or buckle. A further development of the same idea is to be seen in the

---

[1] Cf. J. Riolanus, *Anthropographia* (Parisiis, 1626), p. 286 ; G. Franckius, *Satyrae medicae XX* (Lipsiae, 1722), p. 41 ; M. Schurig, *Parthenologia* (Dresdae & Lipsiae, 1729), p. 370, etc.

sewing up of the vulva, either in the child or in the fully developed woman, an instance of the latter occurring in England as late as the eighteenth century.[1]

In the course of our brief survey of the history of the chastity belt we shall pass in review a few of the mechanical methods which have been devised and employed in various parts of the world to ensure chastity and virtue in the female. But we shall not discuss in any detail these devices in this book. The essay here presented is concerned solely with the use of the girdle of chastity, and other methods will only be mentioned in so far as they throw light upon the history and development of the belt as we know it to-day.

The Girdle of Chastity (French, *Ceinture de Chasteté; Ceinture de Virginité; Serrure de Jalousie*, etc. German, *Brüch, Schloss; Italianischer Schloss; Keuschheitsgürtel; Keuschheitswächter; Venusband; Treuschutz; Weiberverschluss; Jungfernschloss; Jungfrauengürtel; Schloss der Eifersuchtigen*, etc. Italian, *Cintura di castità; Freno della lasciva*.[2] Dutch, *Kuischheidsgordel*, etc.) consists essentially of two main parts : a band of flexible metal and a perforated

[1] E. J. Dingwall, *op. cit.*, p. 59.
[2] Cf. S. Legati, *Museo Cospiano annesso a quello del famoso U. Aldrovandi* . . . (Bologna, 1677), Lib. iii, cap. xvi, p. 253.

4

plate or pair of hinged plates. The band is worn around the body above the hips, the hinder portion passing just above the nates. The second part of the apparatus, if in one portion, is attached by a joint to the flexible band in front. This second piece, constructed either of metal, bone, or ivory, is made convex so that it presses firmly against the mons veneris and extending downwards completely encloses the vulva, a dentated or plain perforation permitting the natural functions but being too small to admit even the tip of the finger (see Pl. VII, p. 96). When two plates are used these are hinged or jointed in the middle, one section covering the anterior portion of the body, whilst the other is drawn up in a posterior direction cóvering the natal cleft and attached to the band where it passes just above the buttocks. In this case the lock can either be in the encircling band or at the back where the hinged plate joins it. In the former one-piece model the lock is usually in front, the band being made adjustable in both cases to fit persons of varying degrees of girth.

In the cases where two plates are used, not only are the external genitals guarded, but also the anus, this precaution being taken, so report has it, in order to prevent those variations in the methods of coitus which were said to have been introduced into Italy from the East. [1]

Generally speaking these are the two main forms of the girdle of chastity. Variations exist, as we shall have occasion later to observe, and methods of adjustment, locking devices,[2] and padding vary according to country of origin and individual idiosyncracies. Thus the girdle in its true form is merely a simple device mechanically to prevent illicit coitus and auto-erotic satisfaction and has nothing in common with those methods which involve a direct mutilation of the genital organs.[3]

[1] In this connection one recalls the obscene lines of Baffo which, it is said, were compiled on the occasion of the visit of the Duke of York to Venice. On this occasion jealous husbands thought of applying girdles to their wives. Baffo writes:

No digo, che sto Duca sia un santon,
Eche nol sia portà per el chiavar,
Se alla mona gà tutti devozion.
Ma che le vacche s'abbia a lucchettar,
Ve zuro, che no vedo oltra rason,
Sol, perchè le se fazza buzarar.

G. Baffo, *Raccolta universale delle opere di G. Baffo* (4 vols., Cosmopoli, 1789), vol. ii, p. 46.

[2] Cf. C. de Pauw, *Recherches philosophiques sur les Américains* (2 vols., Berlin, 1768-9), vol. ii, p. 142; J. G. Krünitz, *Œconomische Encyclopädie, oder allgemeines System der Land-Haus- und Staadts-Wirthschaft . . .*, (242 Thl., Berlin, 1773-1858), Th. cxlvi (Berl., 1827), under Schloss d. Cardan: *Eros oder Wörterbuch über die Physiologie . . .* (2 vols., Stuttgart, 1849), vol. i, p. 619.

[3] Similar devices have occasionally been used in the case of males. One was on exhibition in Berlin in the spring of 1906 and it seems probable that this was the specimen from the Kaiserin-Friedrich Haus Collection (P. Noury, *Les entraves mécaniques à la fonction de reproduction* (Chron. Méd., Paris, 1906, xiii, 610-11), p. 611); F. M. Feldhaus, *Die Technik der Vorzeit, der geschichtlichen Zeit und der Naturvölker* (Leipzig and Berlin, 1914), 564 ff.; E. and J. de Goncourt, *Journal* (9 vols., Paris, 1887-96), vol. vi, pp. 146-7.

INTRODUCTION

For many years controversy has been raised
concerning the reality of the girdle of chastity
as an instrument which has been truly employed
as a preservative of female continence. The
existence of such devices could not be doubted,
but grave suspicion attaches to many of the
specimens extant, and it has been thought in
some quarters that all have been made as erotic
mystifications from specifications to be found
in the literature both of France and Italy and
in order to satisfy the collectors of the curious.
Such speculations as these could only have
arisen among persons imperfectly acquainted
with the facts. They could not have been
seriously discussed if some consideration had
been paid to the origin, history, and purpose of
the girdle of chastity. Unfortunately even now
our knowledge of the early history of these belts
is singularly meagre. Although they have been
commonly reported as dating from mediaeval
times, Dr. G. G. Coulton assures me that he
personally knows of no earlier specimens than
those in the Cluny Museum in Paris, and
similarly Dr. Eileen Power appears not to have
come across any mention of them in her studies
of the lives of mediaeval women. Indeed the
whole of the existing literature is not abundant,
and the majority of the critical notices are
ill-informed and rely too much on the testimony

of former writers. One difficulty which besets the inquirer is the rarity of those sources of information which, if examined, might furnish the student with the materials required. The secrecy with which erotic literature is guarded in our great libraries makes it a task of some magnitude to examine in any way fully those out-of-the-way works where references to such objects as girdles of chastity might reasonably be expected to be found. I have done my best to indicate briefly in the notes where such information is to be gleaned, and take here the opportunity of thanking the curators of the reserved sections of such collections as are to be found in London and Paris, Berlin and New York, Philadelphia and Harvard for the help they have given me in permitting me access to these somewhat rare books. Nevertheless, the information derived is hardly worth the search involved. The detailed history of the girdle of chastity does not seem to have been recorded. All we can do is to gather up the scattered threads as they occur, and try to obtain some clear idea of the general picture as it is found preserved in book and manuscript, engraving and newspaper from decade to decade. Moreover, a summary of a selection from the literature will not be without value to the English student, since up to the present time no survey of the whole field has been attempted in our language.[1]

[1] Slight sketches in foreign languages are : E. M., *Le Cinture di castità : notizie storiche* (Roma, 1881), of which it seems later editions were published in Milan in 1883 and again in Rome in 1887 and which has been attributed to Valerio Busnelli ; Dr. Caufeynon [*pseud.*, i.e. J. Fauconney], *La ceinture de chasteté : son histoire, son emploi, autrefois et aujourd'hui* (Paris, 1904) : F. Grapow, *Der Keuschheitsgürtel* (Geschlecht und Gesellschaft, 1911, vi, 289–307).

CHAPTER II

HISTORICAL SURVEY

As we have already observed in the introduction the root idea of the girdle of chastity is extremely simple. But it was many centuries before it took the form of the flexible metal covering, and in the meantime there may have been simpler kinds apart altogether from the barbarous expedient of infibulation, or the actual sewing up of the labia majora.[1]

From the knowledge at present at our disposal it does not seem probable that the custom of female infibulation arose in Europe. It seems more likely that it originated in the East, and Africa has been suggested as its birthplace. However that may be, the custom, I think, does not appear in Greek or Roman life, and the virgin girdles of antiquity have nothing in common with the chastity belts, although certain of the customs clustering around the use of these sashes suggest ideas allied to the notion of a forcible closure of the private parts.[2]

---

[1] Cf. A. Bordier, *Des mutilations ethniques* (Annales de l'enseign. sup. de Grenoble, 1893), p. 17.

[2] Cf. A. Tola-Paix (*Actualités.*) *Les Ceintures qui parlent* (Paris, 1861),

Indeed the adoption of a belt or even a more elaborate form of dress has long been indicative of a desire to preserve chastity, and such devices are found distributed in many parts of the world. For example among certain of the gipsy women in Spain, where chastity is highly prized until marriage, and where bodily purity (*lácha ye trupos*) is one of the most esteemed of virtues, it would appear that the girls are occasionally forced to wear tied around the loins a sort of handkerchief clout which is now and then inspected for signs of illicit disarrangement.[1] Similarly Pallas reports that among the Circassian girls the custom is sometimes found of providing them, between the ages of ten and twelve, with laced stays or even a broad girdle of untanned leather. This is passed tightly around the loins and sewn up in the case of poorer maidens, whilst their richer sisters have it secured by means of silver locks. This belt is worn until marriage, on the night of which the bridegroom cuts it with a sharp dagger, a proceeding which, it is

p. 10; F. Fiedler, *Antike erotische Bildwerke in Houbens römischen Antiquarium zu Xanten* (Xanten, 1839), p. 19; W. J. Dilling, *Girdles: their origin and development* (Caledonian Med. Journ., 1913, 337–57, 403–25; W. J. Dilling, *Girdles, their use in obstetric practice* (Proc. XVII Intern. Cong. Med., 1913, Sect. xxiii), p. 69.
[1] See W. Simson, *A History of the Gipsies* . . . (London, 1865), p. 257; G. Borrow, *The Zincali* (London, 1901), pp. 267, 382, 391; and cf. V. Areco, *Das Liebesleben der Zigeuner* (Leipzig, 1910), pp. 34, 188, 259, 273.

11

reported, is not infrequently attended with some danger.[1]

Again it is said that rather similar precautions are sometimes taken by suspicious husbands in Eastern and Northern Europe. Stern reports that such customs are not unknown in parts of Poland, and he also states that certain of the Samoyed men are so jealous of the chastity of their wives that they employ a kind of girdle to secure it,[2] an opinion which does not seem to be shared by such authorities as Schrenck, who for his part declares that infidelity is an everyday occurrence in both sexes. [3]

In Africa, where the practice of female infibulation has a certain vogue especially in the Sudan and elsewhere, the use of the girdle of chastity has not, as far as I am aware, been widely reported, although writers, in dealing with infibulation, have not failed to observe the identical ideas at the root of both practices.[4] It would seem that the former custom is associated with a culture of a lower grade than that in which the girdle of chastity flourishes. Just

[1] P. S. Pallas, *Travels through the southern provinces of the Russian Empire in the years* 1793 *and* 1794 (2 vols., London, 1812), vol. i, pp. 398–9; cf. X . . ., *De l'usage de l'infibulation dans l'antiquité et dans les temps modernes* (Union méd., Paris, 1847, i), p. 610.

[2] B. Stern, *Geschichte der öffentliche Sittlichkeit in Russland* (2 vols., Berlin, 1907–20), vol. ii, pp. 428, 502.

[3] A. G. Schrenck, *Reise nach dem Nordosten des europäischen Russlands* (2 pts., Dorpat, 1848–54), vol. i, p. 479.

[4] Cf. the excellent account in F. Jousseaume's *Impressions de voyage en Apharras* (2 vols., Paris, 1914), vol. ii, pp. 33–48, 403 ff., 509–10.

as in modern times in, for example, Europe, female infibulation appears to be confined to the lower strata of society, so are girdles of chastity supplied only to the upper classes, who can afford such luxuries, and who are aware that bodily cruelty is punished more heavily than the imposition of mental torture. In Samoa a method has been employed which, it is feared, would hardly prove efficacious in a more civilized community.[1] It merely consists in using a yellow paint. This substance is extracted from the *ago* plant (*Curcuma longa* L.) which is daubed on the woman's forehead, belly, and arm-pits when the husband goes on a journey.[2] Whatever may be the experience of those using this method it does not seem to have become widely diffused. At any rate a much more drastic device was formerly in use in N. Celebes, which perhaps suggests European influence. Here an actual jointed girdle was employed provided with lock and key thus closely resembling the models to which we have become accustomed in the West.[3]

[1] Cf. La Fontaine's amusing tale, "Le Bât" (*Œuvres*, Paris, 1883-92, vol. v, 227-30).

[2] See A. Krämer, *Die Samoa-Inseln* (2 vols., Stuttgart, 1902-3), vol. ii, pp. 274-6 ; B. Schidlof, *Das Sexualleben der Australier und Ozeanier* (Leipzig, 1908), p. 301. Among the Croats a much more barbarous method has been reported : see F. S. Krauss, *Die Mittel zur Verhinderung des Beischlafes* (Anthropophyteia, 1906, iii), p. 252.

[3] J. H. van Boudyck-Bastiaanse, *Voyages faits dans les Moluques, à la nouvelle Guinée et à Célèbes* . . . (Paris, 1845, pp. 123-4). A simple curved plate has been reported to be used in Bolivia, but I am not satisfied that the evidence is conclusive.

13

In the above examples a few selected instances have been described which will give the reader some idea of certain of the devices which have been used in different parts of the world in order to preserve the purity and virtue of woman. They have, however (with the exception of the device said to have been employed in Celebes), little connection with the girdle of chastity, and hence, since the present study is primarily concerned with that invention, it will not be profitable further to consider them. We must pass on to the history of the chastity belt in the form in which we know it to-day, and try to review some of the controversial material which has accumulated regarding its origin and use.

There has been considerable discussion as to the date when the girdle of chastity first appeared in Europe. There can be little doubt that the idea of such a device, at least in a somewhat modified form, was current at least as early as the second half of the twelfth century. In the Guigemar Epic, which exhibits strong traces of Oriental influences, Marie de France (*fl.* 1180) narrates an incident which suggests knowledge of such contrivances. She tells how one day Guigemar was taking leave of his lady and how she told him that if he were killed she herself would no longer desire life. She begs

14

for his shirt as a pledge of fidelity and exacts his promise to plight his troth only to her who could undo it. Thereupon she ties a knot in it and arranges it in such a way that it could only be undone by a stranger by means of cutting or tearing the linen. Then in his turn the knight Guigemar takes a girdle knotted in a peculiar fashion, and ties it around the naked body of his lady, and then she swears only to love him who is able to open it without any force being applied. As the poem puts it :

> Par une cainture autresi,
> Dunt à sa car nuë l'a çaint
> Parmi les flans aukes l'estraint
> Qui la bucle porrat ovrir,
> Sans dépescer è sans crasir,
> Il li prie que celi aint
> Puis l'a baisié ; à-taunt remaint.[1]

This handing over of a pledge of fidelity in the shape of a belt worn around the nude body is certainly suggestive of a girdle of chastity ; and, in spite of the vehement denials of certain authorities, another passage in the *Livre du Voir-Dit* of the fourteenth century poet Guillaume de Machaut can, it seems to me, be construed in this sense. Before discussing

[1] Marie de France, *Poésies* (2 vols., Paris, 1819–20), Guigemar, 569, vol. i, pp. 90–1. Cf. A. Schultz, *Das höfische Leben zur Zeit der Minnesänger* (2 vols., Leipzig, 1879–80), vol. i, p. 595.

the objections it will be well to consider the passage as it stands :

Adont la belle m'acola,
Et mis son bras à mon col ha,
Et je de .II. bras l'acolay,
Et mis son autre à mon col ay :
Si attaingny une clavette
D'or & de main de maistre faite,
Et dist : " Ceste clef porterez,
Amis, & bien la garderez,
Car c'est la clef de mon tresor.
Je vous en fais seigneur des or,
Et desseur tous en serez mestre.
Et si l'aim plus que mon oeil destre,
Car c'est m'onneur, c'est ma richesse,
Et ce dont puis faire largesse.
Par vos dis ne me puet descroistre,
Ainsois ne fait tousdis qu' acroistne."
La clef pris, & li affermay
Dou bien garder, car moult l'amay.
Puis, pris un anel en mon doy,
Et li donnay, faire le doy.
Lors en souspirant congié pris.
De ma douce dame de pris,
Car pour le soleil qui venoit,
De là partir me convenoit.
Si m'en alay les faus menus,
Tant qu'en mon hostel suis venus.[1]

[1] G. de Machaut, *Le Livre du Voir-Dit* (Paris, 1875), pp. 161-2.

Or again, " Et, par especial, de la journée de la beneyçon du Lendit, et de l'eure que vous partistes de moy et je vous baillay ma clavette d'or : si la vueilliés bien garder, car c'est mon trésor plus grant . . . ." [1] Now this poem by Machaut consists essentially of the correspondence and poetry which passed between the writer and the young and noble lady who inspired him in the later part of his life, and who was long supposed to be Agnes of Navarre, but who may have been Perronne d'Armentières. The little golden key which she hands over,

> " Ceste clef porterez,
> Amis, & bien la garderez,
> Car c'est la clef de mon tresor "

may be the pledge of her honour as some editors insist or may be the actual key to a girdle which guarded *sa richesse*. The editors of the edition published by the Société des Bibliophiles françois vigorously deny this latter interpretation,[2] as also does Laborde, who declares that " comme usage établi, ces ceintures n'ont point existé, surtout chez une nation aussi spirituelle que la nôtre . . . Je les rejette

[1] G. de Machaut, *op. cit.*, p. 165.
[2] G. de Machaut, *op. cit.*, p. 162.

17

donc ".[1] This opinion, is, however, not one
which was held by Lacroix, who inclines to the
view that Machaut is speaking of an actual
chastity belt and that his language cannot be
understood to be merely metaphorical.[2] However this may be, and the evidence is not
wholly conclusive in either direction, it does not
seem to be improbable that, in the case of
Marie de France, at least, the existence of the
girdle of chastity is intended. If this be so, then
the use of the device in Europe goes back into
mediaeval times, and the theory of some that
it was introduced into Italy at the time of the
Crusades might be justified.[3] This hypothesis
is certainly attractive if we consider the Oriental
origin of the girdle of chastity, or at least of some
of the more primitive means of preserving
female virtue. The importance of Venice as a
centre for Oriental trade need hardly be
emphasized, and the political relations, not only
of Venice but also of such centres as Pisa and

[1] L. E. S. J. de Laborde, *Notice des émaux exposés dans les galeries du Musée du Louvre* (2 pts., Paris, 1852–3), vol. ii, pp. 197, 525. He states that girdles were first heard of in 1350.

[2] P. Dufour, *Histoire de la prostitution* (8 vols., Paris, 1851–61), vol. v, pp. 271–2.

[3] Cf. H. G. Prutz, *Kulturgeschichte der Kreuzzüge* (Berlin, 1883), p. 46. It would seem that P. Mantegazza (*Gli amori degli Uomini*, 11a ed., 2 vols., Milano, 1892, vol. i, p. 200), Caufeynon (*op. cit.*, p. 3), and B. Bauer (*Wie bist du, Weib ?*, 36ᵉ Aufl., Wien, etc., 1925, p. 270) have favoured this theory of the introduction of the girdle of chastity into Europe. Cf. O. A. Wall, *Sex and sex worship* (London, 1919), pp. 83, 470 ; and E. Fuchs, *Illustrierte Sittengeschichte*, vol. i, p. 334.

Genoa, assisted in the general mingling and absorption of varied cultures. With the return of the Crusaders from the East the sexual customs of the Orient became better known to Western Europe. Through the influence of Byzantium sodomy had spread to the provinces of Asia and had deeply affected Arabian culture. Throughout the Middle Ages it was to be found widely diffused in Oriental lands, and even in England as early as the first half of the twelfth century the custom was known in the higher strata of society, whilst Frankish peoples were much addicted to the practice. Naturally other parts of Europe did not remain free, and Italy was long known as a centre for such customs.[1] Indeed the two-piece girdles may have been the direct result of the introduction of this practice into Italy. There can be little doubt that the device which consisted of the single frontal plate and grid was not made use of by those who suspected or had become familiar with another avenue to sexual satisfaction. The second form, in which the hinder plate had a dentated trefoil grid, could only have been employed by persons of perverted tastes, and the necessity for such a device throws some light upon the moral condition of the female

---

[1] Cf. Prutz, *op. cit.*, p. 128 ; G. Grupp, *Kulturgeschichte des Mittelalters* (6 vols., Paderborn, 1907–25), vols. iii, p. 260, and iv, p. 92, 110, etc.

society of the period. Moreover, this double guard has long been associated with Italian models and it would seem probable that it was introduced at an early period.

The Middle Ages are so often thought of as a time when the evils supposed to be the result of modern civilization found no place, that a consideration of the sexual life of mediaeval peoples is apt to startle some who are unaware of the facts. It is true that we do not possess a great variety of erotic literature belonging to mediaeval times. But the seeds which later were to bear such remarkable fruit at the Renaissance can be detected and the cult of beauty was not lacking in certain of the early poets. Apart altogether from the influence of mariolatry which cannot fail to be seen in the literature of the Troubadours, the theme of *l'amour courtois* was not wholly intellectual. Such poets as, for example, Arnaut de Mareuil, deal with an aspect of physical beauty which it is sometimes hard to disentangle from the purely erotic. In any serious consideration of this matter it will be seen that there are no hard and fast lines which divide the pure from the impure. All such divisions are arbitrary and misleading, and in scientific treatment are out of place and cannot be tolerated. It is true that undue emphasis can be laid upon the purely physical, and it is here perhaps that the artist can make himself felt. For as the Renaissance approached and the courtly love began to give way to a more corporeal worship, so the descriptions of both male and female charms began to become more detailed and alluring. Modesty weakened from stress of desire ; and with the awakening of Europe began the stirring of powerful passions and the corresponding decline in continence, not only in life but also in literature. It was not everywhere like the love of Dante for the blessed Beatrice or of Petrarch for his shadowy Laura.

Some of the Provençal poets were not averse to painting female beauty in a way which gave promise of a richer fulfilment as the years went by.[1]

> Lo cors a blanc, sotil e gai
> Fresca com rosa de mai,

they sang, and the eyes were

> Belhs huels amoros
> Huoills plens de dousor

which shone out like a pair of resplendent gems.

But above all the breasts received a goodly share of praise. *Las teticas agudicas* were much

---

[1] Cf. R .Renier, *Il tipo estetico della donna nel medioevo* (Ancona, 1885), pp. 7, 14, 16, 29.

admired, and then as now the poets sang of
la mamelete dur a sentue et tastée.[1] Marot, in
his famous poem, sums up their virtues in a
way which has scarcely since been equalled,

> Tetin refait, plus blanc qu'un œuf,
> Tetin de satin blanc tout neuf,
> Tetin qui fait honte à la Rose,
> Tetin plus beau que nulle chose,
> Tetin dur, non pas Tetin voire,
> Mais petite boule d'Ivoire,
> Au milieu duquel est assise,
> Une Freze, ou une Cerise,

and in a burst of confidence continues

> Quand on te voit il vient a maints
> Une envie dedans les mains
> De te taster de te tenir.[2]

Even the licentious Baffo, many years later, who,

> Per tutto dove som, e dove vago,
> Sempre davanti i occhj gò la mona [3]

could not but sing of his compassion for Adam,
for

> Se in cima al fatal ramo
> Quei giera i pomi antighi
> Mi compatisso Adamo
> Se l'hà slargà la man.[4]

[1] O. Voigt, *Das Ideal der Schönheit und Hässlichkeit in den altfranzösischen chansons de geste* (Marburg, 1891), p. 49.
[2] C. Marot, *Œuvres* (2 pts., Niort, 1596), pp. 387–8.
[3] G. Baffo, *op. cit.*, vol. i, p. 189.   [4] G. Baffo, *op. cit.*, vol. i, p. 10.

The appreciative movement was not confined to France and Italy. The Minnesingers, who owed a debt to the literature of the Troubadours, joined in the chorus of praise, and their eulogies were not always confined within the bounds of that modesty which certain tastes are wont to prescribe. Just as the nameless poet of the thirteenth century sang so sweetly,

> Le nonbrillet e l'autre chose
> Que Courtoisie nommer n'ose
> Fut si bien fet à sa nature
> Comme il est reson et droiture ;
> Les cuissetes et les jambetes
> Roondes, blanches et crassetes ;
> Les piés petis, orteus menus
> Doivent estre pour biaus tenus.
> Mout fu nature au fere sage
> Qant de vous fit si bel ymage,[1]

so did the old German poets speak of

> Het zway prüstlein als zwo piern,[2]

and describe

> Ir ougen als der stern(e) schîn,
> rôsen var ir wengelin
> Ir kel wîss als ein harm,
> ir vingen klein, sinewel ir arm.[3]

---

[1] R. Renier, *op. cit.*, p. 39.   [2] Renier, *ibid.*, p. 83.
[3] F. H. von der Hagen, *Gesammtabenteuer* (3 vols., Stuttgart and Tübingen, 1850), vol. ii, p. 56 from Zwingäuer's *Der swanger Münch.*

Even the Minnesinger, Tannhauser, in the thirteenth century, did not hesitate to speak of *ir sizzel gedrolle*, and in one piece describes with the ardour of a lover how

Reit brun ist ir meinel.[1]

Moreover the songs of approbation were not confined to the female sex. Male strength and slimness of loin were appreciated by the maidens of the twelfth century just as they are to-day.

Grailes par flans et gros par pis

sang Beaumanoir ; and a white skin and bright eyes were much admired by the ladies of the court.

La car blance con flors de lis,

says the writer of *Floire et Blanchefleur* in the thirteenth century, and Gui de Bourgoyne is not far behind when he sings of the

Char plus blance que argent ne cristal.[2]

---

[1] A. Schultz, *Quid de perfecta corporis humani pulchritudine Germani saeculi XII et XIII senserint* (Vratislaviæ [1866]), p. 18. Cf. M. Bauer, *Das Geschlechtsleben in der deutschen Vergangenheit* (2 Aufl., Leipzig, 1902), pp. 304 ff. ; M. Bauer, *Die deutsche Frau in der Vergangenheit* (Berlin [1907]), pp. 177 ff.

[2] A. L. J. Loubier, *Das Ideal der männlichen Schönheit bei den altfranzösischen Dichtern des XII und XIII Jahrhunderts* (Halle, 1890), pp. 102, 114. Cf. F. Delicado, *La Lozana Andaluza* (2 vols., Paris, 1888), vol. i, p. 19 ; and A. Semerau's appreciation in *Die Kurtisanen der Renaissance* (Berlin, 1914), p. 9. For a modern comparison see Marguerite Burnat-Provins's poems in her *Livre pour toi* (29ᵉ ed., Paris, 1921).

Indeed the body was praised not only as a thing of beauty in itself but as a source of pleasure to others from which an abundant supply of blissful sensations might be drawn. The seat of voluptuousness was in itself a thing of value, for as Baffo afterwards put it,

Le donne gà un tesoro,
Che è maggio assae dell'oro.[1]

It was something to be protected from external violence, and, as a valued possession, it became to the possessor a jealously guarded treasure with which none might meddle. One could not suppose that the body of a woman was her own property. It belonged to her husband, and those who claimed rights over their own were little better than common harlots. Italian jealousy was always notorious, and the state of Italy was such that a girdle for compelling chastity outside some fixed relationship had nothing anomalous about it. The severe penalties which were inflicted on certain offenders in the twelfth and thirteenth centuries throw into sharp relief the details of the sexual life. The prostitution of children by their parents was punished by flogging, branding, and imprisonment,[2] and rape was, of course, often punished by death.

[1] G. Baffo, op. cit., vol. i, p. 14.
[2] P. Molmenti, Venice, its individual growth . . . to the fall of the Republic (3 pts., London, 1906–8), pt. ii, p. 49. Cf. B. Cecchetti, La donna nel medioevo a Venezia (Arch. Veneto, 1886, xxxi), p. 334.

25

In the fourteenth and fifteenth centuries the evils increased. Stringent regulation of prostitution was adopted by the government in Venice, and the activity of harlots was restricted to certain well-defined areas within the city. As early as 1347 a special department of justice was created in Florence (the *esquetor*) for dealing with the assaults offered to lower class women by men in the upper grades of society. Later decrees strengthened the earlier edicts, but the evils persisted [1] and became more pronounced. With the fifteenth century corruption seems to have become deeper. Venice was described as a sink of iniquity, and nothing was said to equal the libertinism of the city.[2] Perversions and the use of ingeniously constructed auto-erotic apparatus were known as early as the end of the fourteenth century, and Sercambi tells a tale, which may well have reflected the actual practices of lascivious nuns.[3] Even members of the famous Venetian family of Nogarola were suspected of Lesbian activities,[4] and the Golden Age offered a picture of sexual variations which it would be hard to excel. Homosexual practices amongst men also were rampant in the urban

[1] E. Rodocanachi, *La femme italienne à l'époque de la Renaissance* (Paris, 1907), pp. 309 ff.
[2] P. Molmenti, *op. cit.*, pt. ii, p. 58; cf. A. T. Limojon de Saint-Didier, *La ville et la république de Venise* (Paris, 1680), p. 356.
[3] G. Sercambi, *Novelle inedite* (Torino, 1889), p. 412.
[4] P. Molmenti, *op. cit.*, pt. ii, p. 59.

areas, and although Rome seems to have been the chief centre, Venice was not far behind. Decrees were ineffectual and examples of open transvestitism were common in the streets. Monasteries and nunneries were both infected. By the end of the fifteenth century sodomy was reported amongst monks,[1] and in the city the prostitutes flourished to an amazing extent :—

> Tutte nue in forme strane,
> Che in diversi atteggiamenti
> Fasse i omeni contenti,[2]

or as " Aretino " puts it,

> E ognun si fotte in le piu leggiadre vie,
> C'ha Ponte-Sisto non sarian credute
> Infra le puttanesche gerarchie.[3]

The Venetian baths (*stufe*), where the barbersurgeons and corn-cutters plied their trade, were centres of debauchery and prostitution,[4] and the demand of women for the peculiar services of male barbers provided not only an incentive for lust but ribald verses for many a licentious pen both at the time and long afterwards.[5]

[1] G. Marcotti, *Donne e monache* (Firenze, 1884), p. 180.
[2] G. Baffo, *op. cit.*, vol. i, p. 24.
[3] P. Aretino, *Les Sonnets luxurieux* (Paris, 1882), pp. 42-3. Cf. A. Semerau, *op. cit.*, p. 153.
[4] G. Marcotti, *op. cit.*, p. 225.
[5] Cf. Poggio's story, *De meretrice conquerente de tonsoris maleficio* (*op. cit.*, cxiv, vol. i, pp. 182-3) and the amusing tale in the *Moyen de Parvenir* (Paris, 1841), Diète xlii, pp. 136-7. For a valuable account of the intimate customs of Italian prostitutes see *Le Zoppino* (Paris, 1883), especially pp. 38-9, and cf. O. Guerrini, *Ricettario galante* (Bologna, 1883).

As time went on Italian jealousy seems to have become such as to cause the decrees to become sterner. The Norcia statutes of the first quarter of the sixteenth century declared that even a simple embrace of a married woman or widow of good reputation was punishable by a heavy fine, and this was sometimes doubled when the victim was a girl and presumably a virgin. At Fermo decapitation even followed such a crime, and it is said that in Naples death was still the punishment as late as 1607.[1] The virtue and purity of women were so closely guarded that prostitutes alone seem to have enjoyed comparative freedom. Even these, however, occasionally succumbed to the entreaties of the seekers after purity. In 1506 it is said that one sermon alone induced eighty-two to be converted, although we do not know how long this sudden desire for continence was sustained.[2]

It was not only in Italy, however, that jealousy was so prominent a feature of social life. With the growing appreciation of the art of exciting the most extreme of voluptuous sensations the hatred of the corresponding temptations began to become manifest. The secretary of Cardinal du Bellay-Langey, François

---

[1] E. Rodocanachi, *op. cit.*, p. 315 ff.

[2] *Zibaldone, notizie, aneddoti* . . . . 1888 [1889], An. i, p. 3.

de Billon, in his rather tedious *Le Fort inexpugnable de l'honneur du sexe femenin* (Paris, 1555), defends women from the vile aspersions cast upon them. Women in Italy, he says, are "les recluses es maisons enfenestrées de double Jalouzye, dont les Freres propres (si j'ose dire) n'osent quelque fois aprocher". And the cause of it all is that "sotte suspicion, Fille de Jalouzie, née en Italye". Women, he declares, are pure and wonderful beings. It is only the sin of men which makes them to be treated as they are. Even their urine "porte en soy merveilleux efficace en diverses choses, quand elle est bien distilée et conjointe aux compositions elémentaires qu'elle requiert selon la Recette de l'Ouvrier ".[1] On the other hand works were not lacking which revealed the other side of the medal. The old saying, *Fœmina, quœ non est fallax, hœc fœmina non est,* seems to have had more supporters than Billon and the men who thought like him. Anti - feminist literature streamed from the presses of all countries, and it does not seem unlikely that they were mainly inspired by the terror of the tempted. For as the fashions changed secret desires were not weakened, but in many cases were made all the

[1] F. Billon, *op. cit.*, pp. 181, 85, 149. Cf. also J. de Marconville, *De la bonté et mauvaistié des femmes* (Paris, 1566), pp. 67 ff., for the incomparable virtue of female urine.

29

more strong. Even in the middle of the sixteenth century the good old times were being lamented, when

> On babilloit soir et matin,
> On baisoit tâtant le tetin,
> On mettoit la main soubz la cotte,
> On tastoit la cuysse et la motte . . .[1]

From the earliest days right through the Middle Ages these books were published,[2] and the hatred and fear of women were voiced in poetry and prose by those who upheld the Christian tradition of the nature of sex and the abomination of its manifestations. "La femme est un animal coleré, instable, lubrique, infidèle et cruel, plus amoureux de chose vaine que de ce qui est certain et asseuré," wrote the author of that fascinating *Tableau des piperies des femmes mondaines* (Cologne, 1685),[3] and the opinion was one which could have been found repeated in a hundred other passages.

[1] *La Complaincte de Monsieur le Cul contre les inventeurs de Vertugalles* (in A. de Montaiglon, *Rec. de poésies françoises des XVe and XVIe siècles*, Paris, 1855, ii, pp. 150–61).

[2] A Wulff, *Die frauenfeindlichen Dichtungen . . . bis zum Ende des 13 Jahrhunderts* (Halle, 1914).

[3] *Op. cit.*, p. 205. One hundred years previously good Brother Estienne had fulminated against the immodest dress of French girls with their "abominables collets, ouuerts & goudronnez" and their breasts open to the public view—"o forfaict insuportable, ô scâdale pernicieux"! (A. E(stienne), *Remonstrance charitable aux dames et damoyselles de France sur leurs ornemens dissolus* (Paris, 1585), pp. 11, 24). The first edition was published about 1570. Cf. L. de Bouvignes, *Miroir de la vanité des femmes mondaines* (Namur, 1684).

Although the infidelity of women was a common source of discussion in every country where love was dealt with in literature, it would seem that in Italy its manifestations were more marked than elsewhere. Even in the seventeenth and eighteenth centuries foreign travellers to that peninsula were amazed at the sexual customs they observed there. Writing in the middle of the seventeenth century, Audeber declared that the kiss amongst the unmarried was a thing " si diffamatoire à la femme, que celle qui a esté baisée " has half lost her honour,[1] and Lassels, a few years later, says that the Italians are so extraordinarily jealous that for the most part married women live miserably,[2] although years later the growth of cicisbeism seems somewhat to have alleviated their lot.

Indeed Sharp, in his travels in Italy in 1765 and 1766, although he remarks upon the hellish wickedness of Venice, regards marital jealousy on the part of the majority of husbands as obsolete. He seems to have looked upon the system of cicisbeism as far from that exercise of Platonic friendship that Baretti[3] insisted

[1] N. Audeber, *Le voyage et observations de plusieurs choses . . . en Italie* (Paris, 1656), pp. 42–3.

[2] R. Lassels, *An Italian voyage, or a complete journey through Italy* (2nd ed., London, 1698), p. 20.

[3] J. Baretti, *An account of the manners and customs of Italy* (2nd ed., 2 vols., London, 1769), vol. i, pp. 79 ff.

that it was. To Sharp it was not at all "an innocent kind of dangling fribble" but an "abominable and infernal custom".[1] How far these opposing views can be reconciled does not concern us here. It is clear that a sharp cleavage is apparent, and enough has been said to show, in the briefest outline, the development and decline of that jealousy which made the girdle of chastity not only possible, but a natural accompaniment of the prevailing culture. Indeed the use of such a device is what would be expected, especially if it arose at a time when returning travellers from the East became acquainted with methods there in use for enforcing female chastity.[2] Moreover, the chastity belt has a decided advantage over the Oriental method. No mutilation is necessary, and the ease with which the apparatus can be removed renders it in every way more convenient than the fixed rings. Hence the adoption of the belt in preference to the more barbarous method was a natural step in the

---

[1] S. Sharp, *Letters from Italy, describing the customs and manners of that country, in the years* 1765 *and* 1766 . . . (2nd ed., London, 1767), pp. 211, 11, 73.

[2] Cf. G. J. A. Witkowski, *La génération humaine* (5ᵉ éd., Paris, 1884), p. 60, who states that Musulmans use them for their wives when they go on short journeys confining infibulation to the times when their absence is likely to be lengthy. P. Broca states in this connection that not only are girdles and other devices used in the East, but that the common mode of infibulation for married women is not the sewing up of the parts but the passing of a ring through the *labia majora*, thus drawing them together (see *Union méd.*, 1864, p. 92).

developmental history of the idea, and the additional advantage of the double protection made its use obligatory upon those who suspected that if one avenue were closed the other might be utilized. However that may be, the evidence seems to lead to the supposition that the girdle of chastity, in the form in which we know it to-day, was introduced into Europe in the twelfth or thirteenth century; that its introduction may have been due to Oriental influences; and that there was nothing incompatible with its use in the sexual life of the men and women of the period.

It is true that it appears that so far no specimens of undoubtedly early date have been discovered. Few, if any, go back to a time anterior to the sixteenth century, and many of those on exhibition are, in my opinion at least, not to be considered as genuine. Apart from actual specimens, however, we possess another source of information, namely representations in early MSS. One of these occurs in Konrad Kyeser von Eichstadt's military encyclopædia, the *Bellifortis*.[1] Kyeser was born, according to his own account, of a noble Frankish family in 1366. He wrote his experiences of the military art in a handsome book containing

[1] See *Verzeichniss der Handschriften im preussischen Staate. Hanover* (3 vols., Berlin, 1893–4), Philos. 63, vol. i, p. 164. The girdle is in the tenth book.

33

one hundred and forty leaves and a great number of illustrations. The MS., dated 1405, is now in the library of the University of Göttingen, and a girdle of chastity is therein figured and described. The drawing shows a complicated piece of apparatus, and it is described as " Florentinarium hoc bracile dominarium, ferreum et durum, ab antea sic reseratum ". It would thus seem that it was made of iron and could be locked, being used on the Florentine women for reasons which are easy to divine.[1] From its appearance the girdle is both clumsy and heavy and has little in common with the later models which served the same purpose (see Pl. II, p. 49).

As an account of an early fifteenth century girdle this note by Kyeser is interesting, and it is possible that other accounts may be preserved elsewhere in MSS. which I have not yet seen commented upon in the various works that I have consulted. Thus it may be said that, as far as our knowledge goes at present, this is the earliest reproduction of a girdle of chastity known, although, as we have seen, Laborde declares that these belts were first heard of as early as 1350, without, however, giving the evidence for this statement.

[1] See A. Schultz, *Deutsches Leben im XIV und XV Jahrhundert* (2 vols., Prag, etc., 1892), vol. i, p. 283. Cf. F. M. Feldhaus, *op. cit.*, 564–5.

As is well known, common report is almost unanimous as regards the origin of the girdle of chastity in Europe. This story is repeated so often and is quoted so extensively that some consideration of it ought to be attempted. I refer of course to the Carrara legend.

Francesco, called Novello Carrara, the Francesco II of the Carrara family, was put to death by the Venetians in 1406. As the tyrant of Padua and as an enemy of Venice for a long period, his name is associated with much cruelty and oppression, and the historical evidence does not seem to be wholly lacking in support of these opinions.[1] Whatever may be the truth of these accusations, the fact remains that the alleged cruelties of Carrara were illustrated in Venice for many years by the exhibition in the small Sale d'Armi in the Ducal Palace of a number of ingenious objects of torture which were said to have been used by the tyrant upon his unfortunate victims. Included amongst them was a girdle of chastity which rumour and tradition insisted had been used by him to enforce chastity upon his mistresses. The history of these objects is obscure, and Berchet, in his sketch of the history of the small armoury, has not succeeded in tracing it in detail. Both the *golziera* (iron

---

[1] Cf. *Cambridge Modern History*, vol. i, p. 266.

collar) and the *luchetto* (girdle of chastity) are discussed, and it would seem that in 1799 one or both were sent to the Arsenal Museum,[1] although the Conservator of the Museo Storico Navale at Venice tells me that the girdle has now been returned to the armoury museum in the Ducal Palace.

There can be no doubt that this chastity belt has been in Venice for centuries, and various travellers have reported seeing it in the course of their sight-seeing expeditions in the city. Unfortunately many of the most observant critics either did not visit the small armoury, or, if they did so, failed to remark upon the girdle which was on exhibition there. Thus Coryat in his spirited account of Venice did not visit the armoury at all since he was unable to obtain the special permit which

---

[1] F. Berchet, *Le Sale d'Armi del Consiglio dei Dieci nel Palazzo Ducale* (Atti d. R. Ist. Ven. d. Sci., Lett., & Arti, 1899–1900, lix, pt. 2 (ser. 8, ii), pp. 157, 181). The girdle itself consists of the usual hip band, padded on the inside and divided into twenty jointed pieces. To the centre piece in front is hinged another short joint to which in turn is attached the frontal plate with its opening for enclosing the vulva. This orifice is surrounded at its edges by a set of thirty-six projecting teeth, and at its lower end the plate is hinged to another, circular in shape with orifice studded with fifteen teeth. To this anal plate is secured a strip of five jointed pieces, the end of the last being provided with three slots for adjustable attachment to the hip band behind, of which one end is similarly provided, the other being fitted with the staple for the padlock. See Plates III and IV which I owe to the courtesy of the Director of the Palazzo Ducale at Venice, and to whom I here tender my cordial thanks. Cf. U. Nebbio, *Le Sale d'Armi del Consiglio dei Dieci nel Palazzo Ducale di Venezia* (Bergamo, 1923), p. 80.

was apparently necessary.[1] But his observations on Venetian society and his account of certain of the twenty thousand courtesans who populated this " Paradise of Venus "[2] make his work a valuable picture of the sexual life of the time. Almost all the women, he says, " walke abroad with their breastes all naked, and many of them have their backes also naked even almost to the middle, which some do cover with a slight linnen, as cobwebbe laune, or such other thinne stuff : a fashion me thinkes very uncivill and unseemely, especially if the beholder might plainly see them."[3] Such sights he considers very unsuitable, being merely an "incentive and fomentation of luxurious desires ". On the other hand, as Billon had previously observed,[4] married women were kept secluded and cooped up within their houses, the proverbial Italian jealousy preventing them from enjoying the same liberty which was habitual to their sisters of lighter virtue.

Again John Evelyn, who was in Venice in 1645, actually visited "the Private Armorie of the Palace ", but unfortunately left no account of what he saw therein [5] and conse-

[1] T. Coryat, *Coryat's Crudities* (2 vols., Glasgow, 1905), vol. i, p. 345.
[2] T. Coryat, *op. cit.*, vol. i, p. 402.
[3] T. Coryat, *op. cit.*, vol. i, p. 399. Cf. B. Ritter, *Nuditäten im Mittelalter* (Jahrb. f. Wiss. u. Kunst, 1855, iii, p. 229).
[4] F. de Billon, *op. cit.*, p. 181.
[5] J. Evelyn, *Diary* (4 vols., London, 1906), vol. i, p. 242.

quently no mention of any of those stories or current gossip concerning the girdle of chastity. Similarly Liverdys, who wrote an account of a journey in France and Italy, which he published in Paris in 1667, describes the armoury and the " coulier de fer dont il [i.e. Carrara] se servoit pour faire mourir les hommes ",[1] but makes no mention of the girdle. Hence it would seem that about 1667 the story was current that the iron collar preserved in the Palace was a relic of Carrara, and it is possible that, since it had been for some reason associated with the girdle, the latter was also considered the invention of the Paduan oppressor. The same thing seems also to have occurred on the visit of Richard Lassels, the first edition of whose book on Italy was published in 1670. He gives a careful description of the little arsenal and mentions the " Chollar of Iron of the Paduan tyrant (as they call him here) Carara ".[2] But although he touches upon the other instruments of torture associated with Carrara he does not say one word on the girdle and its supposed association with him, an omission made also by Huguetan, whose book on his Italian travels was published in 1681.[3]

[1] *Journal d'un voyage de France et d'Italie* [by B. G. de Liverdys] (Paris, 1667), pp. 828–9.

[2] R. Lassels, *op. cit.*, p. 245.

[3] J. Huguetan, *Voyage d'Italie curieux et nouveau* . . . (Lyon, 1681), p. 210.

On the other hand, Colbert, who appears to have been in Italy some ten years earlier, says that in the small arsenal were " beaucoup d'autres choses ou fabuleuses ou ridicules " besides those which he mentions, and among the former it is quite possible were included the girdle of chastity.[1]

Eight years, however, after the publication of Huguetan's volume François Maximilien Misson published the first edition of his book on his observations in Italy. Although in some respects he is a credulous writer there is no reason to suppose that he made statements which he knew were untrue. In his account of the little armoury he describes the various articles of torture which were said to have been used by Carrara, including a little toilet box, the opening of which caused an explosion, and also he says that " ibi etiam sunt serae, et varia repagula, quibis turpe illud Monstrum, pellices suas occludebat ",[2] a statement quaintly rendered into English in the 1695 edition by " there are also Locks, and sundry kinds of Bolts, with which that beastly Monster lock'd up his Whores ".[3] There can be little doubt, I think, that Misson

---

[1] J. B. Colbert, *L'Italie en* 1671 (Paris, 1867), p. 225.

[2] F. M. Misson, *Nouveau voyage d'Italie fait en l'année* 1688 (2 pts., La Haye, 1691), pt. i, p. 162.

[3] F. M. Misson, *A new voyage to Italy* (2 vols., London, 1695), vol. i, p. 169.

is referring to the girdle of chastity, and it is a pity that he did not make careful inquiries as to the source of the tale that the apparatus had been used or invented by Carrara. But Misson was not the man to make inquiries on the spot and doubt the words of his informants. Yet it is curious that other authors did not seem to care to mention the odd instrument which was on view in the Ducal Palace. Thus Mirabal, in his account of his amorous intrigues in Venice and his references to the jealousy of Italian husbands, might have been expected to mention Carrara's girdle when he visited the small arsenal, but he does not do so,[1] and similarly Mr. Speaker William Bromley is silent, although he declared that the private arsenal " is full of so many curiosities that it ought to be seen ",[2] thus whetting our appetites for details and giving us nothing. On the other hand, C. F. Einckel discusses the collection and mentions the " Schloss, welches dieses Monstrum seiner Gemahlin vor die Natur gemacht ".[3]

In a consideration of these authors it will be seen how none assist us in a solution of the

[1] N. Mirabal, *Voyage d'Italie et de Grèce* . . . (Paris, 1698), p. 21.
[2] *Several Years Travels through Portugal, Spain, Italy, Germany* . . . *and the United Provinces* (London, 1702), p. 212. Cf. E. Veryard, *An Account of Divers Choice Remarks* . . . (London, 1701), p. 129.
[3] C. F. Neickelius [i.e. C. F. Einckel], *Museographia* (Leipzig und Breslau, 1727), p. 119.

reason why this girdle, preserved in the small armoury of the Palace of St. Mark in Venice, was supposed to have been invented and used by Francesco Carrara. Charles de Brosses, the first President of the Burgundian Parliament, and a man of simple tastes and abundant good humour, visited the museum sometime between 1739 and 1740. He saw the girdle and repeats that the " machine odieuse " was devised by Carrara and was used " pour mettre en sûreté l'honneur de sa femme ", adding sardonically that " il falloit que cette femme eût bien de l'honneur, car la serrure est diablement large ".[1]

Nearly fifty years after de Brosses visited the armoury and nearly a century after the Carrara legend had become established, appeared Part 37 of the great German encyclopædia of J. G. Krünitz. This volume makes some mention of girdles of chastity and states that " in Italy a certain chastity lock is well known, of which the inventor was the late Tyrant of Padua, Alexius Carrara ", and the article goes on to say that in Spain also such belts were employed.[2]

I am not aware of the origin of the story that Alexius Carrara was the inventor of the girdle

[1] C. de Brosses, Lettres familières . . . (Paris, 1858), Lettre xvi, p. 137.
[2] J. G. Krünitz, op. cit., Th. 37 (Berlin, 1786), pp. 191 ff. Cf. J. T. Jablonsky, Allgemeines Lexicon der Künste und Wissenschaften (Königsberg und Leipzig, 1767), I, 700b.

of chastity, neither have I discovered any good evidence that there ever was an Alexius in the Carrara family.[1] From the statement that it was the tyrant of Padua who was the inventor it would seem certain that the writer of the article in the Krünitz encyclopædia meant the Francesco Carrara of history, although it is not easy to understand how he got the real character mixed up with a legendary person by name Alexius. Nevertheless the tale has passed into general circulation and the later encyclopædia of Ersch and Gruber repeat it without taking the trouble to verify so easily an ascertainable fact.[2] It is unfortunate also that Maier, in his detailed guide to Venice published between 1795 and 1796, omits to mention both the iron collar and the girdle in the little arsenal,[3] although Zanotto, in his account of the Ducal Palace, speaks of the " serratura di ferro, o meglio ostacolo " which was used by Francesco Carrara on account of his " strana gelosia ", thus giving no support to the German story of Alexius Carrara.[4] Similarly Henri Fleury, in

[1] P. Litta, *Celebri famiglie italiane* (Milano, 1819–58), vol. i, fasc. xxii (Milano, 1831), Carraresi di Padova.
[2] J. S. Ersch and J. G. Gruber, *Allgemeine Encyclopädie der Wissenschaften und Künste* (Leipzig, 1818–50), Ier Sect. G (1851), Th. 52 ; Galanterie, p. 284.
[3] J. C. Maier, *Beschreibung von Venedig* (4 pts., Leipzig, 1795–6), pt. i, pp. 208 ff.
[4] F. Zanotto, *Il Palazzo Ducale di Venezia* (4 vols., Venezia, 1841–61), vol. ii, pt. xix, 5.

his account of his observations in Italy, records visiting the arsenal and seeing various instruments of torture used by Carrara. He states that one of the most singular is assuredly the *Ostacolo*, which Brosses (as it seemed to him wrongly) joked about, and which shows how far human folly can extend when left free to follow its own whims. This monstrous apparatus, he continues, was devised by the ferocious jealousy of the husband in order to ensure the material fidelity of the wife, and made her who was subject to it a victim of permanent and truly atrocious torture.[1]

From the above remarks it will be seen that the Carrara legend has persisted down the centuries, and how there does not seem to have been any good evidence to support it. It would appear possible that the girdle may have been originally acquired together with the instruments of torture which have become associated with it, and, since they seem to have been found together,[2] the story of their invention by Carrara arose on account of the hatred of the Venetians for him and of the stories of barbarism which were inseparably linked with his memory. At any rate the report seems to be legendary,

[1] H. Fleury, *En Italie* (Vienne, 1861), pp. 290–1. Cf. J. Davenport, *Aphrodisiacs and Anti-aphrodisiacs* (London, 1869), p. 144, and J. A. Dulaure, *Des divinités génératrices* (Paris, 1885), pp. 266.

[2] F. Berchet, *op. cit.*, p. 159.

THE GIRDLE OF CHASTITY

and later writers would do well to dismiss it
unless they are able to adduce substantial
evidence in its support.[1]

We have seen above how tradition records
the introduction of the girdle of chastity into
Italy. The story of its appearance in France
is very different. Lacroix sums up the matter
succinctly when he writes, " Rien n'est mieux
établi que le fait de cette introduction d'une
mode italienne, qui existait surtout à Venise
depuis plusieurs siècles et qui y était venue
d'Orient. Il est probable que les croisades
avaient également importé en France un usage
odieux, qui ne pouvait se concilier avec le
respect que nos ancêtres portaient aux dames.
Cet usage remontaient néanmoins à la plus
haute antiquité, et il avait pu se perpétuer des
peuples dont la religion maintenait l'esclavage
de la femme." [2] It will be seen how Lacroix
believes that the origin of the custom is to be
sought in the East and how its introduction into
Europe may have been brought about through
the return of the Crusaders from their expeditions. It will also be noted that he thinks that
we have good evidence for the story of how the
Italian girdles were introduced into France,

---

[1] Even the usually well-informed Bonneau styles Carrara the oldest
European historical character in connection with the girdles of chastity
(A. Bonneau, *Curiosa* (Paris, 1887), p. 228).
[2] P. Dufour, *op. cit.*, vol. v, p. 271.

and, although the tale has been told before, it will bear re-telling in this place. Pierre de Bourdeilles, Abbé de Brantôme, who flourished in the middle of the sixteenth century and died early in the seventeenth, was a writer of wit and brilliance, who did not fail to observe and describe the follies of his age. In his *Les Vies des Dames galantes* he gives us a long series of anecdotes concerning the sexual manners and customs of the times, relating incidents filled with such intimate details that the work has unfortunately received a reputation for lubricity that it scarcely deserves. Much of the material is valuable when considering the social fabric of the period as it is seen reflected in the lives of certain restricted classes, and the psychological details of amorous activity prove that Brantôme himself had a profound appreciation of the technique of *ars amandi*.

In the course of his narrative, Brantôme tells the story of the introduction of the girdles of chastity into France. He says : "Du temps du roy Henry, il y eut un certain quinquailleur (dealer in metal goods) qui apporta une douzaine de certains engins à la foire de Sainct-Germain pour brider le cas des femmes, qui estoyent faits de fer et ceinturoyent comme une ceinture, et venoyent à prendre par le bas et se fermer

45

en clef ; si subtilement faits, qu'il n'estoit pas
possible que la femme, en estant bridée une
fois, s'en pust jamais prévaloir pour ce doux
plaisir, n'ayant que quelques petits trous menus
pour servir à pisser. On dit qu'il eut quelque
cinq ou six maris jaloux fascheux, qui en
acheptèrent (bought) et en bridèrent leurs
femmes de telle façon qu'elles purent bien dire :
' Adieu, bon temps.' Si en y eut-il une qui
s'advisa de s'accoster d'un serrurier fort subtil
en son art, à qui ayant monstré ledit engin, et
le sien et tout, son mary estant allé dehors aux
champs, il y applicqua si bien son esprit qu'il
forgea une fausse clef, que la dame l'ouvroit
et le fermoit à toute heure et quand elle vouloit.
Le mary n'y trouva jamais rien à dire. Et
se donna son saoul de ce bon plaisir, en dépit
du fat jaloux cocu de mary, pensant vivre
tousjours en franchise de cocuage. Mais ce
meschant serrurier qui fit la fausse clef, gasta
tout ; et se fit mieux, à ce qu'on dit, car ce
fut le premier qui en tasta et le fit cornard :
aussi n'avoit-il danger, car Vénus, qui fut la
plus belle femme et putain du monde, avoit
Vulcain, forgeron et serrurier, pour mary, lequel
estoit un fort vilain, salle, boiteux, et très-laid.

" On dit bien plus : qu'il y eut beaucoup de
gallants honnestes gentilshommes de la cour
qui menacèrent de telle facon le quinquaillier

que, s'il se mesloit jamais de porter telles
ravauderies (stupid nonsense), qu'on le tueroit,
et qu'il n'y retournast plus et jettast tous les
autres qui estoyent restez dans le retrait (down
the drain); ce qu'il fit; et depuis onc n'en
fut parlé. Dont il fut bien sage, car c'estoit
assez pour faire perdre la moitié du monde, à
faute de ne le peupler, par tels brindements,
serrures et fermoirs de nature, abominables
et détestables ennemis de la multiplication
humaine." [1]

How far this account can be called historical
we have no means of knowing. It is always
difficult to say if Brantôme's stories are true,
although it is probable that the majority of
them are founded on something better than the
mere invention of the author. There does not
seem any inherent impossibility in the story,
and, apart from Brantôme's sly remarks on the
population problem, the tale is straightforward
and may be founded on fact. However that
may be, we possess other evidence that girdles
of chastity were known in France early in the
seventeenth century and had been probably
introduced before that date. In Tallemant Des
Réaux's *Les Historiettes* occurs a remark which
indicates the possible use of such a girdle,

[1] P. de Bourdeilles, Abbé de Brantôme, *Œuvres complètes* (11 vols., Paris, 1864–82), vol. ix, pp. 133–4.

although I have not found any confirmation of the statement elsewhere.

Gédéon Tallemant, Sieur Des Réaux, was born in 1619, and adopted a legal profession, becoming in due course *conseiller de parlement* in Paris. But his literary tastes were not in accordance with his legal profession, and by a prudent marriage he allied himself with the Hôtel de Rambouillet. This step opened up for him a brilliant field of observation, which, as time went on, he utilized to the full. His anecdotes are full of the gossip and scandal of the times, and although he gives rein to his malicious wit it does not appear that he has ever been charged with persistent inaccuracy or misrepresentation.

In one of the volumes of his history he mentions a certain Nicolas le Jay, who, apparently towards 1630, had been appointed to the Presidency of the Parliament of Paris. He declares that, on a certain occasion the President was " sollicité par une jolie personne, qui feignoit que son mari étoit si jaloux, qu'en allant il lui avoit mis un brayer de fer ; cela enflamma le président : le brayer n'étoit pas si fermé qu'on ne le pût reculer, mais le bon homme y gagna une vache à lait. C'étoit une malice qu'on lui faisait ".[1] We have no means

---

[1] G. Tallemant, Sieur Des Réaux, *op. cit.* (10 vols., Paris, 1861), vol. x, p. 32.

Plate I

est florentinanun licet gracile dianum
ferrn et diun, ab antea sic restatun

Induracio ferri icp blanq piam riber et vidio
ain ad plantii videlz delana cor abrasa cet
salis cuis ad sitmitatem dim fiat z extinghic
in lic copostto i

Plate II

of knowing if the President ever had this remarkable experience, but doubtless his " precedentes dignitez " and his " eminentes qualitez "[1] supported him in dealing with so embarrassing a situation. At any rate the use of the girdle continued to be reported and sometimes in the highest circles of society. For instance, Jean Buvat, in his *Regency Journal,* tells of how such a device was actually forced upon Charlotte Aglaé d'Orléans, commonly called Mlle. de Valois, who married the Prince of Modena. She was born in 1700 and her married life does not seem to have been a happy one. Her husband was narrow-minded, egotistical, and suspicious, and it is possible that these characteristics favoured his treatment of his wife as it is recorded by Buvat. The marriage could scarcely have been successful. Writing to her father, Mlle. de Valois, or rather the Princess of Modena, declares herself the most unfortunate creature in the world seeing on every side nothing but grief and despair. After her marriage it is said that she wept for three days and neither ate nor slept,[2] and it would certainly seem that the character of her husband was one which could easily give rise to scandalous

[1] M. Gaultier [*Ode à M. le Jay* (Paris, 1631 ?)], iii.
[2] E. de Barthélemy, *Les Filles du Régent* (2 vols., Paris, 1874), vol. i, p. 370, and vol. ii, p. 41. Cf. C. E. de Savoie-Carignan, *Six Great Princesses* (London [1913]), p. 237.

stories and outrageous suspicions. With regard to the story of the girdle of chastity, I quote Buvat's account as it is preserved in a MS. in the Bibliothèque Nationale in Paris, since in Campardon's edition of the *Journal* the details of the apparatus are omitted.

" On disait aussi, par avance, que la jalousie ne manquerait pas d'obliger la Princesse, peu après son arrivée à Modène, à se soumettre à la loi que cette passion insupportable y a établie, aussi bien que dans les autres cours d'Italie, et même parmi les personnes d'un rang moins distingué, qui est de porter une espèce de cadenat fermant à clef et dont le mari garde scrupuleusement la clef. C'est comme une Ceinture de velours qui envelope les reins et les cuisses de la Femme, afin que le Cadenat soit également soutenu et appliqué directement sur sa partie, de sorte qu'elle se trouve entièrement masquée, en ne lui laissant que l'ouverture nécessaire, quand elle a besoin d'uriner, pour la sortie de l'Eau." [1]

[1] J. Buvat, *Journal de la Régence* (1715–23) (2 vols, Paris, 1845), vol. ii, pp. 28–9 (19 fév., 1720) ; MS. (Fond franc.), 10283 (Bib. Nat., *Cat. gén. des MSS. fr., Anc. Suppl. fr.* (Paris, 1896), ii, p. 87), Tome iii, p. 1179. The story is also told that one of the girdles in the Cluny Museum (No. 6598) was used by Henri II for Catherine de'Medici, but the size of the girdle apparently proves the incorrectness of the report. See Bonneau, *op. cit.*, p. 232 ; H. N. Williams, *Henri II, his court and times* (London (1910)), p. 309.

Another version of the same legend asserts, if we can believe E. M., the anonymous author of *Le cinture di castità* (Roma, 1887), p. 24, that this girdle was made for Anne of Austria, wife of Louis XIII, and was

From what Buvat states in the above extract it is clear that the use of the girdle was not unknown to him. Indeed, if we can accept his words it would appear that these belts were known to be often used in Italian society circles even amongst those of high rank. However that may be, the apparatus he describes is not quite the same as what would have been expected from the specimens in our museums. Instead of being a steel plate secured to flexible jointed bands passing round the body, this consisted rather of a broad velvet band encircling both the loins and thighs. To this band was probably attached a curved plate fitted with the necessary dentated aperture which, passing between the legs, was firmly pressed against the vulva.

Similarly in Germany the use of the girdle seems not to have been unknown. One of the early pictorial representations is the woodcut, published first, I think, in the 1572 Bâle edition of Sebastian Brant's famous work *Das Narrenschiff* (The Ship of Fools).[1] In it is told the tale

worn by her. The same author quotes from an alleged thirteenth century chronicle which states that the girdle of chastity was known at the time of the Albigensian Crusade, but I have not succeeded in tracing this reference or confirming the identity of the prior " Oddone di Faix ", who is one of the characters in the story. Another fact which is given in this work, although without any references, is that the girdle of chastity was condemned in the Courts of Love, especially that presided over by " Eleonora di Sciampagna ".

[1] S. Brant, *Stultifera Navis mortalium* . . . (Basileæ (1572)).

51

of the fool who protected the locusts from the sun ; of the fool who pours water into a well ; and of the fool who tries to protect by force the virtue of his wife. The woodcut in the first (1494) edition of the work shows in the foreground a man in a fool's garb pouring water into a well ; whilst to his right is another who is apparently engaged in washing and polishing some bricks. In the background stands a third fool protecting a swarm of insects with a heavy stick, and further back a woman is depicted leaning out of the window of a strong lock-up.[1]

In the German version of 1574 a change occurred in the woodcut,[2] but this had previously appeared in the Bâle edition of 1572. The German version reads :—

DER XXXII NARR

Der hüt der Heuwschreck [3] an der Sonn |
Und schüttet wasser in der Bronn |
Wer hütet das sein Frauw bleib from̄.

The poem then continues :—

Von Frauwen hüten

Viel Narren tag und selten gut |
Hat wer seiner Frauwen hüten thut |

---

[1] S. Brant, *Das narre schyeff* (Nuremberg, 1494).
[2] S. Brant, *Welt-Spiegel, oder Narren Schiff* (Basel, 1574), p. 115 v°.
[3] Locust.

Denn welch wol wil | die thut selb recht |
Welch ubel wil | die macht bald schlecht.
Wie sie zu wegenbring all tag |
Ir böss fürnemmen und anschlag |
Legt man ein Maulschloss schon darfür . . .

The woodcut illustrating the poem shows to
the left in the foreground a fool pouring water
into a well, whilst to his left is a nude woman
seated upon a block and partly hidden behind
a curtain. Girt about her waist is a belt and in
her left hand she holds a chain from which
is suspended a stout padlock, whilst just beyond
the curtain is another fool brandishing a staff
at some locusts. On a slope in the background
to the left another naked girl is lying. This
woodcut does not appear in the German versions
published in 1497, 1545, 1549, 1560 and 1566,
neither is it the one published in the Paris editions
in 1507 and 1513. Nor does it appear in the
Antwerp edition of 1584, where the earlier form
is seen, another type of which appeared in the
edition of 1625 published in Franckfurdt am
Mayn.

It will be noted that, in the early form of
the woodcut, the woman is closely confined in
a castle or lock up, whilst in the later form
she is seated secured by a chain and heavy
padlock. Yet before the cut was changed the

text described how " legt man ein Maulschloss schon darfür ", etc. This Maulschloss (Malschloss, Malchslosz, Mahlenschlosse, *O.H.G.*, Malaha, Mantica, etc.) is, properly speaking, a padlock for luggage, but as early as 1590 it seems to have been employed by Fischart in his edition of Gargantua in the sense of a girdle of chastity, or at any rate of a padlock securing such a girdle. He is speaking of the cunning and wiles of women and says, " Ach was ist über weibergelüst und list, da helfen keine beschnittene kämmerling, noch panzerfleck (steel plate [1]) mit mahlschlossen ",[2] a passage which certainly suggests such a girdle or steel plate which is secured by a padlock. The same idea may then have been present in the mind of the artist, when the early woodcut was changed, and the later form depicted a woman wearing a belt and holding a chain and heavy padlock.

As the years went by the use of the girdle of chastity became more and more widely known in Germany as elsewhere. In 1781 appeared a little book on infanticide by Karl Müller, which I have not found in any medical library up to the present time, and the contents of which I know only through the quotations

[1] Properly a metal piece used in repairing a cuirass.
[2] F. Rabelais, *Affentheurlich Naupengeheurliche Geschichtklitterung, von Thaten und Rahten der . . . Helden und Herren Grandguisier, Gargantoa . . .* (Gänsserich [i.e. Strasburg], 1590), cap. i, p. 47.

of others. It appears to be one of those manuals which denounced the evils of masturbation in the children of the period who were accustomed to be represented as monsters who were bringing themselves to the asylum or even the grave on account of their vicious practices. In my *Male Infibulation*[1] I mentioned some of these manuals in connection with the infibulation of boys, but it would appear that girls indulged themselves just as much as their brothers, and similar forcible means had to be adopted to restrain them. One of these methods seems to have been the imposition of apparatus which resembles girdles of chastity.

Müller's girdle[2] consists of a thin, flexible steel band passing round the body. This band is about as thin as the spring in an ordinary clock, and is so light and flexible that, although it has the strength of a band of moderate toughness, it has also the great advantage of being comfortable in such conditions as that of a full stomach or of constipation. This band is covered with leather or padded with some other material, and in front is provided with a

---

[1] E. J. Dingwall, *op. cit.*, p. 54.
[2] K. Müller, *Mittel wider den Kindermord* (Halle, 1781). The quotation is taken from J. G. Krünitz, *op. cit.*, Th. 31 (Berlin, 1784), pp. 763 ff. A very similar account was published in 1795 in *Zeichen und Wert der verletzen und unverletzen Jungfrauschaft*, which formed Pt. I of *Gynäologie oder das Geschlechtsleben in seinem ganzen Umfange* (16 pts. in 8 vols., Stuttgart, 1843); see vol. i, pp. 145 ff. of this edition.

little lock which is so arranged that it also securely fastens the piece, which, in the form of an arc, passes between the legs. This is united behind with the waist band, and passing between the legs divides over the anus forming an oval slit, and then immediately joining again. Over the vulva it is connected with a suitably arranged plate of brass which is bent round convexly and is provided with the necessary opening. From this point the arc is brought upwards over the stomach and unites with the waist band, the portion in front as well as behind being covered with some padding material. This means of preventing our daughters from exciting themselves and of preserving their virginity does not seem to have lasted very long. Doubtless there are some households where children are still tortured by the inventions of perverted parents, but it would seem that even in those families where the sexual functions are still regarded as diabolical, and where children are supposed to be especially liable to attacks by the Evil One, these complicated pieces of apparatus are discarded in favour of such devices as long shirts and chemises without an opening![1]

In the middle of the eighteenth century, however, things were different. The girdle

---

[1] A. E[schbach], *Disputationes physiologica-theologicae* (Parisiis, 1884), p. 499.

was not a curiosity only to be found in cases in the basements of museums or in covered show stands hidden away from prying eyes. It seems to have been worn by maidens of the period, but, if we can trust to the author of the *Méschanceté des Filles*, which seems to have been published in the early years of the eighteenth century, they were quite capable of getting friendly locksmiths to provide them with duplicate keys.

This charming book is a lament concerning the moral condition of the girls of the period. It might have been written yesterday by a Sunday school teacher and gives a vivid and amusing picture of the smart young ladies of the period. The author complains that girls are only looking for pleasure and no longer wish to remain under the subjection of their parents and of those who have charge of them. If they are punished by being kept indoors they become thin with big eyes and sad, dismal faces, refusing to eat or even to talk.[1] But towards nightfall they begin to wake up. Having got hold of the servants in order to prevent them from telling their parents, they softly leave their rooms and slip out into the night. They do this in order to " talk with their boy friends, to sing and stuff themselves with dainties like

[1] *La Méschanceté des Filles* (Troyes, 1720), p. 7.

fruits, pastry, sugar-plums, preserves and other things ", and when they get back they do not forget the maid who has kept the door open for their return.[1] On the next day, however, they plead headaches as an excuse for not getting up, and on Sundays, even if they do go to Church they spend the time in gossiping and listening to the improper stories which their boy friends tell them, whom they also permit to kiss them on various parts of the body, to feel them and to pay them much attention and flattery.[2] If on the other hand their mothers want them to go out with them they are immediately ill with pains in the stomach which compel them to stay indoors ; or they find they have no suitable neckwear or collars for going out in the streets.[3] They invariably prefer improper stories to the words of a good preacher, and try to get hold of all the indecent literature they can lay hands on, keeping such books much more willingly than catechisms. Among these dangerous books is the *Moyen de Parvenir*, of which they are very fond, and others equally subversive of the morals of young people. As to the care of their persons, they would much rather live on bread and water than not have their bodies well adorned, and their partiality to wine makes the danger to their

[1] *Ibid.*, p. 8.　　[2] *Ibid.*, p. 10.　　[3] *Ibid.*, p. 25.

souls even greater. For wine is the very " Milk of Venus ", and the proximity of the belly to certain other parts is apt to lead the drinker to be more easily corrupted than her temperate sister.[1] Indeed, according to the author of this delightful tract the maidens of his times were as naughty as they could well be, and it is not difficult to imagine one of these festive young things getting her boy friend to bring her a whole bundle of keys to rid herself of the girdle of chastity which her prudent mother had imposed upon her.[2]

[1] *Ibid.*, pp. 35–7.

[2] The *Moyen de Parvenir*, which the author of *La Méschanceté des Filles* mentions as one of the books which were popular among the maidens of his times, was originally published towards the beginning of the seventeenth century. It has been attributed to Béroalde de Verville, who was born in the middle of the sixteenth century, and who was the author of a number of books which to-day are almost forgotten. It consists in the main of a collection of anecdotes, stories, and facetious tales, some of which are dull but others amusing and extremely witty. A great many of the stories would be called indecent to-day, and some would not be understood without knowledge of the customs of the times. It is clear that the girls of the period could not have been very innocent if they enjoyed the *Moyen de Parvenir*. Such tales as the test for a girl's virginity (xxii, *op. cit.*, p. 58) ; the incident of the barber (*op. cit.*, xlii, pp. 136–7) ; and the three brides' account of their husbands (*op. cit.*, lxxxiii, pp. 300–1) are not those which would appeal to the virtuous but which would doubtless have been discussed with peals of laughter over the sugar-plums and pastry.

The times do not seem to have changed so much after all. In the *Evening Star* of Washington, D.C., on 28th December, 1929, appeared an appealing letter from a mother asking advice as to how " to keep our children jollied and in love with their parents ". She complains that her daughter is impudent to a colossal degree and " sasses " her with impunity. What is to be done with such a case ? And the writer who deals with these delicate matters for the *Evening Star* declares that she feels for this poor insulted mother. " If I had some recipe," she writes, " for turning the modern, impertinent, ungrateful, unappreciative girl into a loving, considerate daughter, I could work a miracle

THE GIRDLE OF CHASTITY

A picture of one of these girdles is to be found in the *Frauenzimmerschule*, which is said by Max Bauer to have been published in 1792, but a copy of which I have not seen. The account would seem to have been a translation from Chorier, although it may be that a similar piece of apparatus is being described in both cases. It consisted of a small grille made of gold which was fastened to four small chains covered with thick velvet. Two of these secured it in front and two behind. The other ends of the chain were secured to a band passing round the hips and this was kept together by a lock controlled by a small key. The grille itself was 6 inches long and 3 inches broad, so that it completely covered the genital organs, and it was composed of three little bars which were just separated enough to permit free passage for the urine, but were not wide

that would stanch millions of mothers' tears and lighten the burden that breaks millions of mothers' hearts . . . Nobody knows how to deal with these egotistic, arrogant young upstarts. They are too old to be given the spanking which they so richly deserve . . . They consider their parents doddering imbeciles whose views are too antiquated and senile even to be worth listening to." Oh wicked maidens of America ! Even the Holy Father protests. In his customary address to the chosen preachers of Lent on 4th March, 1930, the Pope lamented the conduct of Italian boys and girls. They follow their own devices ; go about when and how they like, and even send one another invitations wherein the presence of their parents is referred to as " troublesome luggage ". The young people of the world seem to be determined to enjoy themselves in spite of the selfish and futile attempts of their elders to repress them. They go on their way rejoicing, leaving their pastors and masters with bitter feelings born of a rankling choler engendered by the memories of their own lost youth.

enough even to admit the tip of the little finger.[1]

It will be seen from the above that this device is again of the simple " one piece " variety, and from the account it would seem that the upper part of the plate containing the grille rested upon the mons veneris, whilst the lower portion was made convex, the posterior point resting against the perineum. A similar invention, devised by the Scottish surgeon John Moodie in the nineteenth century, will be described later ; here it will be sufficient to indicate the variety of types found in other parts of Europe.

It has been reported, although I know not on what good authority, that a device somewhat akin to that described in the *Frauenzimmerschule* was at one time worn by certain young novices in Peruvian nunneries, and this was imposed upon them as a penance. The apparatus is described as a kind of iron wire girdle (*Drahtgürtel*) and was probably worn in the same way as other inventions of the kind.[2] Neumann states that this custom is recorded

---

[1] *Die Frauenzimmerschule* (1792), p. 182, quoted by M. Bauer, *Liebesleben in deutschen Vergangenheit* (Berlin, 1924), p. 57. Cf. A. Schultz, *Alltagsleben einer deutschen Frau zu Anfang des achtzehnten Jahrhunderts* (Leipzig, 1890), p. 127 ; J. Scherr, *Deutsche Kultur- und Sittengeschichte* (Berlin (1927)), pp. 193–5 ; M. Bauer, *Deutscher Frauenspiegel* (2 vols., München und Berlin, 1917), vol. i, pp. 182 ff.

[2] E. von Bibra, *Reiseskizzen und Novellen* (4 vols., Leipzig, 1864), vol. iii, p. 144.

in certain of the picaresque novels of Spain, but I am not aware to which he is alluding.[1]

As we have said, one method of learning something of the girdle of chastity is to pay attention to the woodcuts and engravings which illustrate the apparatus and its use. The motive of jealousy and the ineffectual nature of bolts and bars provided ample material for the artist, and there are several examples which are worth careful consideration in this place.

One of the most interesting of these is an early woodcut which has been attributed both to Peter Flötner [2] and to Hans Baldung (Grün), but which is now believed to be the work of H. Vogtherr.[3] The woodcut shows a woman, naked with the exception of a girdle of chastity, a necklace and a light head-dress, who is standing between two men. The man on her right is the older of the two and is presumably intended to be her husband. With his left hand he caresses her left shoulder, while his right rests just above her right breast. The

[1] R. K. Neumann, in *Der Sexual-Probleme*, 1912, pp. 267–8.

[2] E. Fuchs, *Illustrierte Sittengeschichte*, etc., vol. i, p. 232; cf. G. Hirth, *Kulturgeschichtliches Bilderbuch* (6 vols., Leipzig und München [1881–90]), vol. i, p. 240, fig. 379, who describes it as by an unknown master; G. Jung, *Die Geschlechtsmoral des deutschen Weibes im Mittelalter* (Leipzig [1921]), p. 120; J. Scherr, *op. cit.*, p. 195.

[3] Dr. F. M. Feldhaus tells me in a private letter that the authorities in the Cabinet of Engravings in Berlin ascribe the woodcut to Hans Baldung (Grün), but it has been suggested with good evidence that it is by Vogtherr (see M. Geisberg, *Bilder-Katalog zu M. Geisberg* (München (1930)), No. 1470, p. 253).

man on the left of the woman is holding out to her a large key, which is obviously one which will fit the heavy padlock attached to the girdle on her right side. His right hand is extended, and the girl is dropping pieces of money into it with her left, whilst her right is engaged in taking pieces of money from a wallet which is suspended from a belt around her husband. The girdle of chastity which the girl is wearing is of simple type and consists of a one- or two-piece belt passing round the body and broadening out before it extends between the legs, doubtless uniting with the upper part of the belt behind. On the right of the belt and at the side is a stout staple through which is passed a heavy padlock in order to secure the girdle round the body.

The woman is saying :—

Es hilft kain shloss für frauwen list
kain trew mag sein dar lieb nit ist
Darumb ain schlüssel, der mir gefelt
Den wöl ich kauffen umb dein gelt,

which can be paraphrased as follows : "No lock is of avail against the cunning of women ; there can be no fidelity where love is not present : for that reason will I buy with your money the key which I lack."

These words are apparently addressed to her

husband, reproaching him with his suspicions and pointing out that force is of no avail against the wiles of woman where there is no love between the partners. The husband says :—

> Gelt und gütz gnung wil ich dir geben
> Wiltü nach meinen willen leben
> Greift mitter hannd in meiner tasschen
> Des sloss will ich dich auch erlassen.

"Money and goods enough I will give to thee if only thou wilt live according to my wishes. Put thy hand into my pocket ; moreover I will let thee off the lock."

The man on the left says to her :—

> Ich drag ein Slüssel zw solliche slossen
> Wie wol es manchen hat verdrossen
> Der hat der narren kappen fill
> Der rechte lieb erkaüffen will.

"I carry a key for such locks, as indeed has vexed many. He who wants to use a bribe to buy the right kind of love has a fool's cap on his head ! "[1]

Taken as a whole the woodcut is finely executed. The expressions on the faces of the three persons are well shown, and the idea behind the scene is well worked out. Moreover, the girdle is of interest as it shows what the

[1] See E. Fuchs, *Ill. Sittengeschichte*, etc., Beilage, vol. i, p. 232. I am not in agreement with Fuch's interpretations on p. 340.

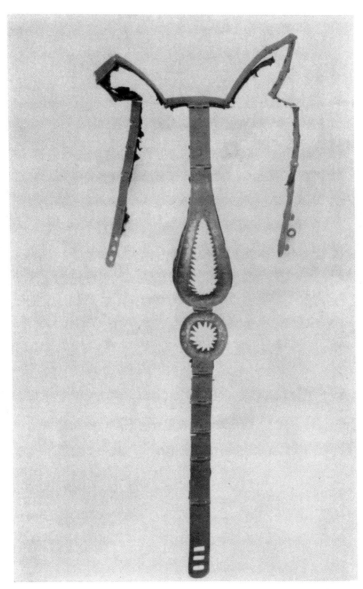

Plate III

Plate IV

specimens must have looked like when they were complete with their velvet coverings. Another representation of a girdle which may be compared with the one described and which, like the former, may date from the sixteenth century, is that to be found in the book-plate of Melchior Schedel, who was a member of the famous Nuremberg family of that name. Melchior himself, who was born in the first decade of the sixteenth century and died towards 1572, does not seem to have left many records behind him. His book-plate, which appears to be known from a copy in a book of late sixteenth century date, is reminiscent of Amman's work, but which has not yet been proved to be by the hand of that master. It is 36·2 cm. in height and 24·7 cm. broad, and the figure on the left is that of a woman, almost naked, wearing a girdle of chastity, and carrying in her right hand a large key and in her left a bag of money. This particular girdle is very similar to that portrayed in Vogtherr's woodcut, only that the padlock is worn on the left of the belt instead of on the right.[1]

A further example of a representation of female perversity and cunning relative to the

[1] See Fuchs, *Ill. Sittengeschichte*, etc., vol. i, p. 197 ; A. Schmidt, *Zwei unbekannte Bücherzeichen des XVI Jahrhunderts in der Grossherzlichen Hofbibliothek zu Darmstadt* (Ztschr. für Bücherfreunde, Jahrg. i, 1897–8, ii, 474–9) ; G. A. Will, *Der Nürnbergischen Münz-Belustigungen* 1er (4er)., *Th.* Altdorf, 1764–7), pt. iv, pp. 89–96.

use of the girdle of chastity is the scene, which is found in varied versions, and which is said by Niel to be in the style of Leonard Gaultier (1552–1641) and to have possible reference to Henri IV and his amours with the Marquise de Verneuil. In a French version it is called " Répresentation du coqu jaloux qui porte la clef et sa femme la surrur ". At the foot of a large bed a woman is seated, a man standing in front of her. To the latter she is presenting a large key, presumably that belonging to the stout and heavy padlock which secures a girdle of chastity around her naked body. Hidden behind the curtains of the bed and to the left of the woman her lover is seen holding a purse to pay for the duplicate key which the woman's maid is holding out to him. To the right in the foreground a fool is trying to keep a swarm of insects in a basket, and to the left a cat is watching a mouse.[1]

In the Cabinet of Engravings in Leyden another version of this is preserved which is said to date from about 1590. On the upper margin are these lines :—

Wie jalours syn wil die siet vry my
Want hier meucht ghy sien wat die jaloursheyt sy

[1] P. G. J. Niel, *Portraits des personnages français les plus illustres du XVIᵉ siècle* (2 sér., Paris, 1848–6), sér. i, n. 6, Henri IV, p. 3.

Daerom vorhaer wil U wachten ghy
Want al hebt ghy een vrouken schoon en
  gracieux daer by
En wilt U daerom in geen jaloursheyt begeuen
Want ghy maeckt U selven maer suur het
  leuen
Maer wilt U vroukens het heure gheuen
So meucht ghy onbevreest met heur in
  vreuchden leuen,[1]

which can be translated thus :—

" Who proposes to be jealous, let him see
me unhindered ; for here ye may see what
jealousy is. For that reason you will guard
yourselves against it ; for though you have a
pretty little wife and a gracious one you will
not on that account have recourse to jealousy.
For you merely make your own life bitter.
But if you will give little wives their due, you
may live with them fearlessly and joyfully."

On the lower margin are the following
verses, which, in almost identical form are found
in a German version of the seventeenth century :

Wer Eÿffern wil der schaw hie an.
Wie es geht fast eim jedern Mann.
Ich sag für war füer Frawen list.
Uff Erden nichts verborgen ist.
Es hatt ein Mann ein Fräwlein schon.

[1] C. E. Daniëls, *Iets over kuischeidsgordels en nog wat* (Nederl. Tijdschr.
v. Verlosk. en Gynaec., 1890, ii, p. 195).

Der hatt ein reis genom̄en an.
Die weil er aber ein eifferer war.
Macht er ein Bruch von eisen gar.
Darmitt er fromm behielt sein Weib.
Zog er das ihr an ihren Leÿb.
Und heing ein starckes schlos darfür.
Das niemand öffnen soltt die thür.
Nam aüch den schlüssel und zog hin.
Das Weib stach bald ein Esell ihm.
Diweill ein alt Weÿb hinderm Bett
Züm Schloss ein andern Schlüssel hett.

Also der Mann wird gleich gehalten.
Eim Narren der wolt Flöh behalten.
In einem Korb und doch Kunat nitt.
Macht ihm nür müh und arbeÿt mit.
So gehts aüch eim der Eiffern will.
Hat niehts denn angst und sorgen viel.
Dleich wie die Flöh im Korb nicht pleiben.
Also das schloss sein gang wirdt Treiben.

Wann einer wil verschliessn
Da ander mehr drumb wissn
Wie mans auff machen kan.
Musz habn ein solcher man.
Schellen an sein Ohren.
Das er sieht gleich eim Thoren.
Dann ist d'Katz nicht zu Hausz
So hat Ihren lauff die mausz.[1]

[1] E. Fuchs, *Geschichte der erotischen Kunst* (München [1912]), Beilage, p. 200.

These lines can be rendered as follows. They give a clear epitome of what men thought about the girdles of chastity from the days of Brant onwards :—

" Let whoever is jealous look here and see how it happens to almost everyone : I tell you in sooth nothing on earth is hidden from the cunning of a woman. A man who had a fair young wife had to take a journey. But because he was jealous he makes a pair of iron breeches.

" In order that he might keep his wife good he draws them round her body and has a big padlock hanging from them so that no one should open the door. He also takes the key away with him. His wife soon makes an ass of him, for an old woman behind the bed has another key to the lock. So the man is like a fool who tries to keep fleas in a basket and cannot do it. It is only trouble and toil to him ; so it will be to one who wishes to be jealous. He has nothing but trouble and anxiety, for just as the fleas do not remain in the basket, so the lock goes its own way.

" When one is minded to lock up something about which others know how it can be opened, then such a man ought to have bells in his ears since he looks exactly like a fool. In such a case when the cat is not at home the mouse can have its play."

Another version of the same scene is preserved in an engraving which Eduard Fuchs attributes to Paulus Fürst and which he dates provisionally at about 1620. In this case the woman is apparently represented trying to snatch the key from her husband, whereas in the other examples she is meekly handing it over to him. Similarly in the former version the cat is not figured and the warrior's trunk is also absent [1] (see Pl. IV, p. 65).

One of the finest representations of the girdle of chastity in practical use is that found in one of Heinrich Aldegrever's delicate engravings, which is here reproduced in plate I, p. 48 from the copy in the British Museum. A naked young man is shown with his right hand on the shoulder of a girl, nude but for a girdle of chastity. In her right hand she holds what is apparently a key which has, it seems, been handed to her by the boy, who is gazing into her face with an appealing expression. For her part she appears to hesitate, for with her left hand she pushes away the boy's left which holds the key, and on her face there is a look of uncertainty and doubt which is admirably portrayed. The girdle itself is very similar to those we have

[1] E. Fuchs and A. Kind, *Die Weiberherrschaft* (3 vols., München (1913–14)), vol. iii, Abb. 53, p. 43. Another version is preserved in the Dept. des. Estampes at the Bibliothèque Nationale, Paris (Tf. 1,73).

already considered. The lock is on the left side and not enough is shown of the girdle to be able to determine whether it belongs to the one- or two-piece variety.[1]

We have given above a short account of some representative specimens of woodcuts and engravings which show the girdle of chastity as it was thought to be worn. Modern French illustrated journals often refer to the practice and occasionally a drawing is included to illustrate and exemplify the text. Photographs also can be obtained in such places as Paris, Barcelona, or Vienna which show girls naked but for girdles, but these are of no interest to the student and may be passed over. We must proceed to a brief consideration of a few of the specimens which, perhaps, are of some historical interest.

From the reports which have from time to time been made by various authorities it does not appear that the number of girdles in existence is considerable. Apart altogether from the modern nineteenth century specimens, the number of examples in public and private collections has been estimated at some few hundreds, although how many of these are

[1] I have to thank the official photographers of the British Museum for kindly taking the photograph for me in order to reproduce in this place. Mention of the piece will be found in A. Bartsch, *Le Peintre Graveur* (21 vols., Vienne, 1803–21), vol. viii, No. 248, p. 437. It is described here as a "dessein de gaine". As will be seen from the engraving the date is 1532.

genuine I am not prepared to say. C. de Boissieu, who investigated this subject, collected evidence, which showed that even in France the number of local museums possessing specimens was not rare, and he mentions Poitiers, Sens, Rennes, Vannes, Brest, Quimper, Montauban, and Albi as places in which the museums preserve examples. He also states that some are to be found in Venetian collections and that the museums in Madrid have two, of which one is said to have been used by the wife of Philip V, of Spain, although I am not aware whether the story concerns Maria Louisa of Savoy or Elizabeth Farnese of Parma. During his lifetime Boissieu stated that he intended printing his observations, but in spite of some research in Paris and elsewhere, I have not succeeded in tracing this work and do not know if it were written, neither have I been able to trace what became of Boissieu's MSS. and photographs. It is not easy to confirm these statements without much unnecessary labour, and it would appear that some of the specimens mentioned by Boissieu are not in the official catalogues, as for instance in Rennes, where I cannot find any trace of a girdle of chastity in the pages of the museum catalogue.[1]

It is thus very possible that, if the specimens

[1] See C. de Boissieu, in *Interméd. d. cherch. et cur.*, 1901, xliv, 429 ff.

exist, they are hidden away where no access is permitted. This is the case at the British Museum, where one girdle is preserved which was formerly in the George Witt Collection, and an inspection of which I owe to the courtesy of Mr. A. B. Tonnochy. This piece consists of the usual plates and jointed hip belt, but the latter is most certainly modern and was probably

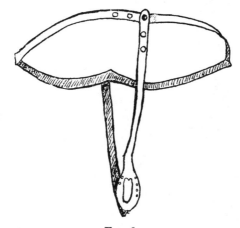

Fɪɢ. 1.

added to the original pieces at a later date. Boissieu states that of the two hundred he has examined two only are pre-Renaissance, and personally I know of no single specimen which can be dated with any degree of certainty as earlier than this. Eduard Fuchs appears to be of the opinion that the specimen in a collection at Poitiers may be of the late fifteenth century,[1] and the authorities of the Wellcome Historical Medical Museum of London assert that a girdle in their collection (No. 7469) dates also from the fifteenth century, although I should be inclined to the view that it is considerably later. This museum possesses three more specimens, of the authenticity of which I cannot assure myself, and the great museum of the Royal College of Surgeons in London also has an example which Dr. C. J. S. Thompson tells me is most certainly geniune, and which, if so, I should date as late sixteenth or early seventeenth century.

Again, before the great fire at the exhibition of waxworks, commonly known as Madame Tussaud's in London, there was an example on view which Fuchs figures in his *Sittengeschichte* and which he dates as from the sixteenth century,[2] but now Mr. Tussaud tells me that it is no longer on exhibition.

The latter part of the sixteenth and the seventeenth centuries seems to provide the greater number of specimens of girdles of chastity, and of these the examples in Germany and Central Europe are perhaps the most interesting. Three of these are in the National Museum in Munich and have been briefly

[1] E. Fuchs, *Ill. Sittengeschichte*, etc., vol. i, p. 190. See Fig. 1, p. 73.
[2] E. Fuchs, *op. cit.*, vol. i, p. 195.

described by Schmid in the catalogue. One (No. 284) is an iron girdle of a circumference of 80 cm., and provisionally dated as from the seventeenth to the eighteenth century, although I think that it is possible that it is very late sixteenth. The hip belt is composed of four iron-jointed bands, and the anterior plate has two openings, one heart-shaped in the lower portions, and above a star-shaped slit. On the edges of the plates are the usual row of small holes for securing the padded covering, and in front are two eyes for attaching a couple of little locks.

No. 285 is another specimen, the hip band in this case consisting of ten jointed strips, the pieces passing between the legs being also jointed. The anterior plate possesses a sharply dentated heart-shaped aperture, the posterior portion being provided with a similarly notched opening. This specimen was once padded with black velvet, but it is in bad condition, having been broken and riveted together. In front there are a couple of revolving eyes through which the round padlocks were fastened, but the latter have been lost.

The third example (No. 286) has a circumference of 82 cm. and is composed of eight jointed iron strips. The anterior and posterior plates, which are also jointed, contain the usual apertures, the one in front being oval with dentated edges, whilst that behind is circular with the rims toothed as before. At one time it appears that this belt was covered with white silk upon the inside and red velvet without, whilst it was secured round the body by a small padlock which was fastened in front.[1]

Perhaps to about the same date are to be ascribed the famous girdles associated with the collection in the great castle at Erbach in the Odenwald. This building, which was reconstructed in the sixteenth century and later restored, contains a number of exhibits of interest such as armour, old firearms, and other antiquities which were brought together by Count Franz von Erbach, who died early in the nineteenth century.

In this collection some girdles are preserved of which one is covered with red velvet but lacks any engraving or other decoration. Another has no covering, although formerly it obviously had such a casing, as the holes drilled at the edges of the plates clearly indicate. The external surfaces of this specimen show a number of etched designs, which are rather crudely executed and are said to be in the style of the sixteenth century.[2] The girdle consists

[1] W. M. Schmid, *Altertümer des Bürgerlichen und Strafrechts* . . . (*Katalog d. bayer. Nationalmuseums*, vii) (München, 1908), pp. 55–6.
[2] Cf. the designs on the Kalmar museum girdle (see Pl. VII).

of a belt, about 1 cm. broad, made of iron and arranged in four jointed portions. Attached to this in front and behind are a couple of narrow metal plates, curved in a convex direction so as to fit the body, and secured to the hip belt by the usual joints. The two plates when in position meet at a point which rests just over the perineum, and are here linked together by another small joint. The posterior plate is perforated at the point which covers the anal region by a trefoil-shaped opening which is about 5·2 cm. broad and 4·5 cm. high. In the girdle, which has no decorations, this hole is circular and of an average diameter of 3·1 cm. The anterior portion is also provided with an opening corresponding in position with the part which covers the vulva. This is a narrow spindle-shaped longitudinal slit, 7 cm. long and 1 cm. broad, the aperture serving the same purpose in the other girdle being 7·6 cm. long and 1·7 cm. broad. In both girdles these openings are furnished with fine teeth along the edges, and in the decorated girdle, placed just above the longitudinal slit, is another opening shaped like an ace of spades.

In this specimen, as has already been said, both plates bear designs which have been etched on their external surfaces. These consist essentially of scroll work which surrounds

77

the designs and inscriptions. The anterior
plate shows at the upper part the figure of a
woman in half profile. She is naked and with
her left hand is seizing the erect brush of a fox
which is in the act of crawling between her

FIG. 2.

FIG. 3.

legs. Beneath the design is the inscription :—

Holt Füxel ich
Hab dich er Wist
Du büst mir Oft dar
Durch Gewist.

78

The meaning of the words is clear, as is also the relation to the design and the girdle. The woman says, "Stop, little fox! I have caught you. You have often been through there!", whilst the lower design amplifies and illustrates the upper. Here, just to the left of the spindle-shaped slit, is the etching of a halberdier standing on guard while the other side is filled in with variegated scrolls (see Figs. 2 and 3, p. 78). On the hinder plate in the upper section is depicted a woman seated on the lap of a man who is facing the observer. His right arm is round her neck and their heads are close together as if in deep conversation. What she is telling him is shown in the inscription which occupies that part of the plate between the design and the trefoil opening. It reads :—

Ach Das sey Eich
geklagt Das mir
Weiber sein mit der
Brüch geblagt,

which can be translated, "Alas, this be my complaint to you, that women are plagued with the [chastity] breeches," a sentiment which is very appropriate if we can judge from the design it is obviously meant to illustrate.[1]

[1] See H. Ploss, M. and P. Bartels, *Das Weib in der Natur- und Völkerkunde*, hrsg. v. Fr. v. Reitzenstein (4 vols., Berlin, 1927), vol. ii, p. 27 ; G. Jung, *op. cit.*, p. 116 ; E. Fuchs, *Ill. Sittengeschichte*, etc., vol. ii, pp. 122–3.

In 1871 two more girdles were discovered in peculiar circumstances in the beer hall of the famous Runkelstein castle near Bolzano. This building was erected in 1237 and attracts many visitors on account of the interesting series of secular wall paintings which give an idea of the decorations which were common in the great castles of medieval times. According to a report by Joseph Kirchner, which is quoted by Pachinger, some members of a small society of historical students were one day at Castle Runkelstein and discovered behind the wainscotting of the beer hall an opening which led to a small lumber room of the existence of which the proprietary tenant had no idea. The chamber, which was little more than a hole scarcely a square metre in extent, was filled with débris and rubbish covered with cobwebs, but among the junk was discovered a couple of old halberds, a long rusty dagger, a broken hunting knife, and a small worm-eaten and half-broken box. In the box, together with a mass of rusty iron fragments and other mouldering material, was found a rather well-preserved girdle, neatly constructed, from the hasp of which still dangled the little heart-shaped padlock, which, however, was unfortunately broken. The piece was well made and showed that it had been constructed by a

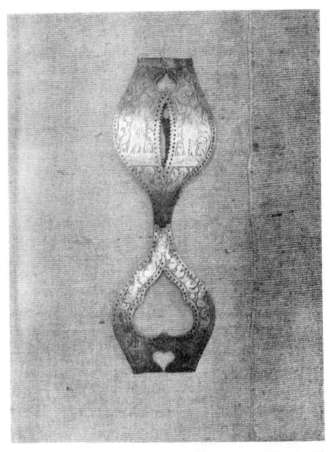

Plate V

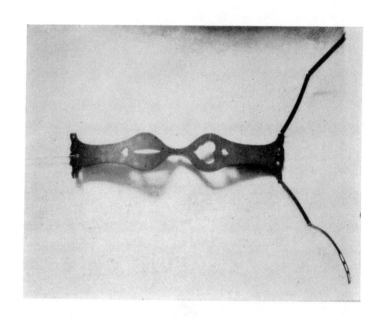

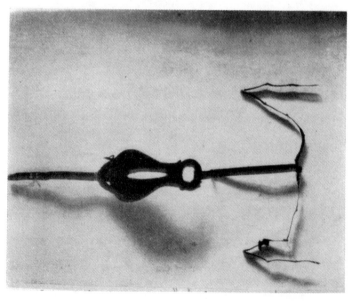

Plate VI

skilled workman. On an underlayer of soft leather attached to the metal plates was still the trace of a former covering of some material, and it appeared that the girdle had also indications of actual use by the previous owner. Besides this specimen the remains of another were discovered, made of adjustable steel plates, but the ravages of rust had been so great that only fragments remained. An offer was made to the tenant to purchase the objects, but he, thinking doubtless that they were worth far more than was proposed, refused, and so they were returned to their old hiding place.[1]

Again in Amsterdam a girdle is preserved which is either late sixteenth century or seventeenth century in date. This example was formerly in the collection of Professor Andreas Bonn (1738-1818) and was presented to the Nederlandsch Museum by one of his descendants. Another specimen, which is now in the obstetric collection of the University of Leyden, is unfortunately defective, but traces of use are apparent and it would seem that in former times it had been covered by a layer of green velvet.[2] Further examples, probably

---

[1] A. M. Pachinger, *Der Keuschheitsgürtel* (Stuttgarter Antiquitäten-Zeitung, 1914, No. 30/33). I quote from the offprint.
[2] C. E. Daniëls, *op. cit.*, p. 192.

of about the same date, are preserved in collections in Vienna, Berlin, Würzburg, and elsewhere, of which Feldhaus has published some
brief account with reproductions in his book,
Die Technik.[1]

It is probable that the best-known girdles
of chastity in existence are those preserved and
on public exhibition in the Cluny Museum in
Paris. They illustrate the two types of girdle
in an admirable manner, and are therefore
often rightly cited as the best examples we have.
The first (No. 6598) consists of a stout steel
band, covered with velvet, and made adjustable
by the simple device of an overlap where the
frontal lock secures the two ends, the two
sections sliding one behind the other and one
being notched for the purpose of fitting into the
locking device. The lock itself is in front and
beneath it is a piece of convex ivory furnished
with a longitudinal oval dentated opening which
in position is pressed firmly against the vulva.
Sommerard, in the Cluny Museum catalogue,
published in 1883, states that this girdle is of
sixteenth century date,[2] but it would seem
that later authorities are of the opinion that
it is early seventeenth century, and I am in

---

[1] F. M. Feldhaus, *op. cit.*, 564 ff.
[2] E. du Sommerard, *Musée des Thermes et de l'Hôtel de Cluny*, Catalogue (Paris, 1883), p. 525.

full agreement with their view in this matter.
(see Pl. VII, b.) The second (No. 6599) girdle is
a finer specimen and is thought to be of German
work of the beginning of the seventeenth
century, or, as some authorities believe, of Italian
manufacture. It consists of two iron plates
jointed together at their narrowest point, to
one of which (the hinder) is attached two jointed
iron bands for passing round the hips and
uniting with the other by means of a couple of
eyes. Both the plates are handsomely engraved,
damascened and picked out in gold. The
anterior portion has, in the usual position, an
oval, or rather spindle-shaped longitudinal
slit, furnished with dentated edges ; and above
is a design showing Adam and Eve in the Garden
of Eden. The hinder plate has a trefoil opening
in the appropriate position, whilst above, the
space is taken up with varied decorations and
arabesque designs. Around the edges both
of the plates and of the hip bands are the usual
rows of drilled holes for the purpose of attaching
the velvet or silk coverings, and the whole
specimen is an excellent example of the well-
made two-piece girdle of chastity. It is said
that this specimen was presented to the Museum
in 1862 by M. Mérimée, but I am not aware of
what its previous history may have been.
(see Pl. VII, a.)

83

From the accounts of a few selected specimens of girdles of chastity which have been given above, it will be seen that no good evidence has been adduced that these objects were ever in actual use by the women of the different periods. For this reason alone the very suggestive circumstances which accompanied the discovery of the famous girdle now in Mr. Pachinger's collection in Munich make it an object of unusual interest.

The girdle was discovered in 1889, when Mr. Pachinger was staying with some relatives in a little provincial town in Upper Austria. At that time restorations were being carried out on the ancient church which had been built towards the middle of the fifteenth century. The sexton was friendly and no objection was raised to Mr. Pachinger joining the group which was engaged on some tedious work. Whilst the excavations had been going on some slabs had to be raised and beneath was found a kind of cavity resembling a strongly walled-in kneading trough. In the space thus revealed they had found a very old leaden coffin, which they hoped to be able to open as soon as possible. Mr. Pachinger fortunately arrived just before the coffin had been opened and was able to be present at the ceremony. The object had been transferred to a corner of the churchyard, and on examination it proved to be a leaden casket, about 1·80 m. long, its dark grey smooth external surfaces showing neither inscriptions nor a coat of arms, whilst the old joints where union of the leaden sheets had been effected were in perfect condition. When the prism-shaped cover of the coffin had been raised after it had been prised open, the first things to be seen were some pieces of rotten wooden boarding which had probably been used for the inner shell. After these had been cleared away the form of the person buried within became visible. The skull was well preserved, and upon it was perched a richly braided coiffure like a wig. The colour of the hair was reddish, and under the rays of the sun it shone like gold. The splendid set of teeth indicated that the deceased had been a young person, and the artistic mode of dressing the hair and also the fine raiment of silk that it was a woman of rank. The skeleton was clothed in a dark brown damask dress, which from its pattern appeared to be of a date of some time after the beginning of the seventeenth century. The arms, crossed over the breast, were sheathed in long leather gloves of a yellowish colour, which reached as far as the elbows. As the skeleton was raised from the crumbling boards on which it rested it was seen that the front parts of the dress alone were well preserved, for the remainder crumbled to dust when disturbed. After the removal of the front part the remains of an apron-like linen shift were disclosed and also those of a short petticoat. Both of these were yellow brown in colour and partly mouldy, so that parts of the ribs and pelvic bones were exposed. When the clothes had been removed and the whole of the skeleton became visible, it was seen that the pelvic bones were surrounded by an iron hoop, jointed in several pieces, and attached in the region of the abdomen to an iron plate the shape of the sole of a shoe, the whole being fitted with a couple of little locks which had almost rusted through. On the surface of the band were the remains of a former sheathing of leather, but this had fallen to dust during the removal of the skeleton. At the back of the body, approximately in the same position as in front, there was another iron plate which had been badly damaged by rust. The anterior portion had been formerly connected with this hinder piece by a joint, which had broken, and, in contradistinction to the posterior plate, was well preserved, even possessing some remnants of the old padding which had been overlaid with a brown or yellow silken fabric. The sexton separated it from the skeleton, remarking that it was a girdle of chastity, and the others would have thrown the pieces away had not Mr. Pachinger begged to be allowed to keep the rusty fragments as a souvenir of the discovery. Unfortunately he did not also preserve the gloves and the few remains of the garment which had survived the ravages of time, and these were flung back together with the bones into a hastily dug grave. The pieces were afterwards submitted to a Munich firm which repaired some of the damage and enabled observers and students to get a clear idea of the girdle as it was when first made with the exception of the padded covering.

In this specimen the hip measurement is 85 cm. ; the frontal plate is 30 cm. long and the hinder plate 31 cm. The jointed pieces vary in length, being from 15 cm. to 4 cm., the average breadth being 1·2 cm. In the centre of the frontal plate is a slit, 7 cm. long and 5 cm. broad, and this aperture is furnished on either side with twenty-one teeth. The posterior plate is thickly coated with rust and in its lower portion has a three-cornered opening which has an average measurement of 3 × 3·5 cm. The iron portions of the hip band are secured to the hinder plate on either side by moveable pieces which are firmly riveted.

The frontal portion is secured to the hip belt by another metal piece to which is attached the device for fastening the padlocks. From its appearance and the circumstances of its discovery, Mr. Pachinger is inclined to date it provisionally as early seventeenth century.[1]

From a consideration of the above it would appear probable that the lady whose skeleton

FIG. 4.

lay in the coffin was one of those cases on whom the burden of wearing a chastity belt had been imposed. It is certainly a pity that Mr. Pachinger did not secure the gloves and the portions of the garment which had not decayed. But there is no reason to doubt the substantial accuracy of his narrative, and I agree with him that this piece is one of the most

[1] A. M. Pachinger, *op. cit.*, see Fig. 4, p. 88.

interesting examples in existence, and trust that he will see that after his death it may pass to some permanent public collection for the benefit of posterity.

From the brief historical survey that I have attempted above it will be seen that there is a direct historical sequence in the fundamental idea which underlies the use of the girdle of chastity. It was observed that there is some reason to suppose that the device of passing a ring or rings through the labia majora had been known for a considerable time in the East, and it was suggested that the idea entered Europe through the influence of returning Crusaders who both modified and improved it. We found in the course of the discussion that civilization had developed in Europe to a point where the use of such an invention for preserving chastity was not in any way opposed to the spirit of the time. The conception of woman as half saint and half devil offered a suitable field for such ideas, and as the years went by and the corruption engendered by the growth of sexual perversities increased, so did the subjection of the married woman increase in proportion as the freedom of the courtesan developed. In noticing certain of the poems of Marie de France and Guillaume de Machaut we remarked that the idea of a girdle of fidelity

89

was not absent, and indeed the actual use of such a girdle may have been intended. Passing on we saw that the earliest representation of a chastity belt so far discovered was that contained in the MS., *Bellifortis*, of Kyeser, which was dated 1405, and in the course of the narrative we found that Carrara of Padua had been credited, according to popular belief, with the invention of the apparatus. Finally we examined a selection of woodcuts and other pictorial representations of girdles, completing our survey by a consideration of some of the extant specimens which led us to the conclusion that few, if any, can be dated with certainty as prior to the Renaissance. In conclusion we discussed the discovery by Mr. A. M. Pachinger of a girdle which was actually in position around the skeleton of a woman who had been interred, it was thought, in the late sixteenth or seventeenth century. This fact suggested strongly that these chastity belts were once worn by women and that the theory that the existing specimens were of the nature of erotic mystifications could not be accepted.

In the next chapter we shall consider the question of the girdle of chastity in relation to the law. It will be shown that the use of the girdle has been the subject of discussion in the law courts, thus strengthening the evidence of the reality of the custom. We shall see how in modern times the imposition of such devices by jealous husbands is proved and thus that the stories of legal proceedings in the past may not be altogether without foundation.

CHAPTER III

THE GIRDLE OF CHASTITY AND THE LAW

IF we assume for the sake of argument that the girdle of chastity has at times been imposed upon unwilling women, it might be expected that cases are on record where the situation has led to proceedings in the courts of law. Indeed, as has been suggested, such cases constitute an important link in the chain of evidence which indicates the reality of the use of this instrument in the hands of the jealous. Were it merely the figment of the imagination of the poet and romancer, the satirist and artist, we should not find it taking its place among the many cruel devices which man's ingenious brain has conceived, used, and finally been forced to discard on account of the legal machinery his less imaginative and more enlightened fellows have constructed.

We do not know for how long woman endured this indignity without a formal and a public protest. Nor to this day do laws exist forbidding the use of the chastity belt. It is only when its adoption becomes an element in a cruel treatment that finally the victim complains and severe retribution is imposed.

Mutual agreement is alone necessary, and for all we know to the contrary there are women to-day who wear girdles of chastity with a perfect willingness born of an infatuation for their jealous mates. However that may be, it is not always so. The famous antiquary Ole Worm tells a story of an incident which seems to have happened towards the middle of the seventeenth century, and to have as a setting " the orchard of Denmark ", or in other words the little island of Falster, south of Sjaelland. At any rate that is where Worm says he first heard the sorry tale.

It appears that in the island there were a married couple with whom things had been going badly for some time. The husband was of an exceedingly jealous disposition, and his suspicions of his wife's fidelity annoyed his friends, who knew that she was chaste and virtuous, an opinion which was shared by all who knew her. Nevertheless her husband treated her brutally and even at times cuffed and struck her. The idea then came to him of insisting on her wearing an apparatus which should ensure her chastity. It consisted of a kind of broad girdle of rough material completely encircling the loins, being provided merely with a slit for the purposes of nature, which could not be opened except by a key.

The whole belt was secured around the body by a strong thong which passed through a number of holes and was thence secured. Thus it was impossible for the poor woman even to answer the calls of nature without demanding the key from her husband, a situation which was sufficiently intolerable. For some months she patiently endured this tyranny, but finally her friends compelled her to take action and have it removed. A party was arranged to which the couple were invited, and when they had all become jovial they reproached the husband with his actions and forced his wife to display the apparatus to the assembled company as she was wearing it under her dress. The husband may then have excused himself, alleging sufficient cause, but the friends of the wife were obviously not satisfied, for the case came up before the court. The husband of the plaintiff was condemned to be banished with ignominy, and the judge ordered him to hand over the key immediately in order to liberate his miserable wife. Finally it seems Worm got possession of the girdle for his museum, where it was exhibited under the caption of *Custodia Pudicitiæ*.[1]

---

[1] O. Worm, *Museum Wormianum seu historia rerum rariorum* . . . (Lugd. Bat., 1655), pp. 388–9 ; cf. M. B. Valentini, *Museum Museorum* (3 pts., Frankfurt am Mäyn, 1704–14), Th. iii, cap. xxi, p. 76.

Probably the most notorious case, however, was that associated with the name of "Freydier, Avocat à Nîmes". This mysterious person has long intrigued the lovers of the curious, and I much regret that all I can do is to raise only a very small corner of the veil which has so long concealed him.

In 1750 a slender volume was published in Montpellier with the attractive title, *Plaidoyer de M. Freydier, Avocat à Nismes, contre l'introduction des cadenats, ou ceintures de chasteté.* It professes to be the speech of the prosecuting counsel at a trial where the use of the girdle of chastity was in question.

According to the report it appeared that a certain Pierre Berlhe was at one time living in Avignon and had as a lodger in his house one M. Lajon who had arranged with Berlhe for his sister, Marie Lajon, to leave Montpellier where she had been staying with some relatives and to come and lodge with him in Avignon. As soon as Sieur Berlhe had set eyes on Mlle. Lajon he became enamoured of her and determined to win her favours. As time went on his passion increased and he courted her ardently, and Mlle Lajon, believing that his wooing was to end in marriage, did not repel him to any great extent. In due course she

95

yielded to her lover, and left with him for a
tour in which she consented to be disguised as
a boy for some reason which is not disclosed.
Their trip took them to Beaucaire, to Montpellier whither they returned for a short time,
and thence to Saint-Gilles and Nîmes, where
she found that she was pregnant and urged
marriage upon her partner. But he postponed
the rite, continually making business an excuse
one day and the necessity of making a journey
the next. On one of these trips he evidently
first thought of a girdle of chastity, for prior
to a journey upon one occasion he fitted
Mlle Lajon with such a belt and locked it with
a padlock. This apparatus consisted of a kind
of metallic corselet secured around the loins
and fastened in front by a small padlock. At
the necessary place a small opening was left
which was surrounded by sharp points and in
different parts of the apparatus were seams
sealed with wax and impressed with a device
which Berlhe kept with the key of the padlock
in his own possession.

After the birth of her child Mlle Lajon was
again forced to suffer the indignity of the girdle,
and Berhle still refused to marry her. Outraged
at the turn things had taken Mlle. Lajon finally
sought relief in the courts and the Plaidoyer is
the account by the prosecuting counsel of her

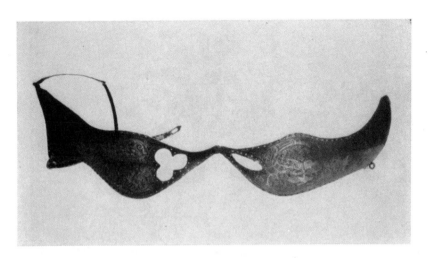

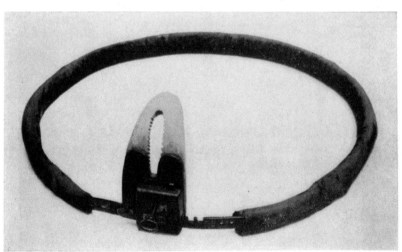

Plate VII

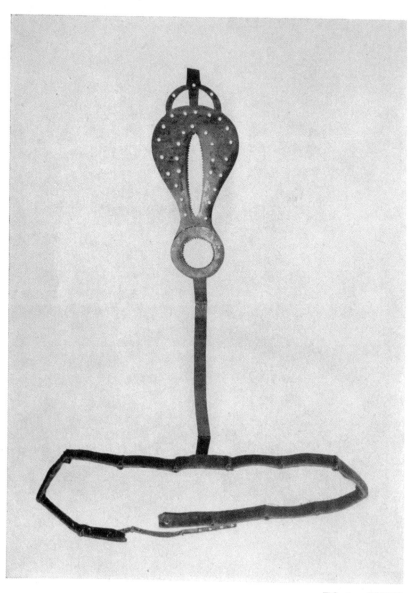

Plate VIII

sufferings and the appeal for sentence against Sieur Berhle.[1]

Now who was Freydier ? The opinion of scholars up till now seems to be divided. On the one hand there have been those who, finding nothing in contemporary literature, memoirs, legal records and letters, have concluded that there was never any such person and the trial is legendary. Among these may perhaps be classed M. Nicolas, who in his literary history of Nîmes, seems to regard the book as a spurious legal record and in addition " à genre badin ".[2] On the other hand, there are those who, although unable to prove the authenticity of the document, are inclined to regard the report as the work of Freydier, whom they consider as an historical person.[3]

This class again may be subdivided into those who consider the document as referring to a real trial, and those who tend rather to the belief that it may be an account of the revival of one of the amusing but vulgar Causes Grasses.

[1] See *Plaidoyer de M. Freydier*, etc. (Montpellier, 1750). This is the first edition. The copy in the British Museum lacks the plate which is found in the copy in the Vallet Collection now in the public library of Montpellier. There have been a number of reprints, of which those of Paris (1863 and 1883) and Montpellier (1870) are the most important. A translation, somewhat abridged, and rendered into English of no great merit ,was printed privately in New York in 1928 and of this edition 645 copies only are said to have been circulated to subscribers.

[2] M. Nicolas, *Histoire littéraire de Nîmes* (3 vols., Nîmes, 1854), vol. ii, p. 230.

[3] Cf. A. Bonneau, *op. cit.*, p. 240.

These were fictitious cases which were argued mainly for amusement and for the burlesque treatment which they offered to the witty orator. They commonly took place on Shrove Tuesday, and the material was almost always of a sexual nature such as cases of adultery or impotence. The custom seems to have fallen into disuse in the early part of the seventeenth century, and I do not know of any revival being subsequently attempted on a large scale.[1] If the Freydier speech was made on such an occasion, we do not seem to possess at present any proof of it. Investigations at Nîmes do not appear to have been fruitful of results of value,[2] but research workers seem to have overlooked one fact which seems to me of some importance.

In the middle of the eighteenth century a certain Antoine Freidier was a " juge des conventions royaux de Nîmes ", and later he was appointed to the Presidial Court, which had been established at Nîmes in 1552.[3] Was this Antoine Freidier the Freydier of the famous Plaidoyer ? It would seem that he might

---

[1] See A. G. Camus, *Lettres sur la profession d'Avocat* (4ᵉ éd., 2 vols., Paris, 1818), vol. i, p. 424 ; A. Cabanès, *Les indiscretions de l'histoire* (3ᵉ sér., Paris, 1906), pp. 31 ff.

[2] Cf. those by Ch. L. writing in the *Int. des chercheurs et curieux*, 1876, ix, 272–3.

[3] L. Ménard, *Histoire civile, ecclésiastique et littéraire de la ville de Nismes* (7 vols., Paris, 1750–8), vol. vi, Succ. chron., p. 12. *Inventaire-Sommaire des Archives communales de Nîmes* (2 vols., Mende [Avignon], 1877–9), E.E. 2, p. 2.

have been, for in 1779 there was published in Nîmes another edition of the Plaidoyer entitled *Le Cadenas : plaidoyer interessant, par M. F.***, avocat au Présidial de Nismes.* Now had Freydier been a fictitious personage it would seem hardly likely that the later edition of his Plaidoyer would have been published with the statement that its author was "*avocat au Présidial*". Moreover cataloguers of the period do not seem to have regarded him as an imaginary character. Amongst the living authors featured in *La France Littéraire* occurs the entry : "*Freydier, avocat à Nîmes, sa patrie,*"[1] and Desessarts repeats the statement in his *Les siècles littéraires de la France.*[2] It is certainly odd that there is no mention of the trial in the *Encyclopédie*, especially as the volume in which it might be expected to appear was published some five years after the first edition of the Plaidoyer saw the light at Montpellier.[3] But the case may not have aroused attention at the time, and even if the editors had heard some talk of it they may not have thought it of sufficient interest to warrant comment in the encyclopædia.

What conclusion then can be drawn from

---

[1] *Op. cit.* (Paris, 1769–84), vol. i, p. 271. J. H. S. Formey in his *La France littéraire* (Berlin, 1757) does not mention Freydier.

[2] N. L. M. Desessarts, *op. cit.* (Paris, An. viii—ix), vol. iii, p. 175.

[3] D. Diderot and J. Le R. d'Alembert, *Encyclopédie* . . . (17 vols., Paris et Neufchastel, 1751–65), vol. xvii, p. 328.

the evidence that we at present possess ? We
have seen that just about the time that the
book containing the alleged speech by Freydier
was published in Montpellier there was a certain
Antoine Freidier resident in Nîmes who was
later appointed to the Presidial Court. And
again it has been pointed out how in Nîmes
in 1779 the Freydier of the Plaidoyer is
described on the title-page of the Nîmes
edition as "*avocat au Présidial de Nismes*".
It is certainly possible that Freydier and
Antoine Freidier are one and the same person,
and it follows that the trial may have actually
taken place and that the Plaidoyer represents
Freidier's speech on that occasion. Moreover
the description of the girdle of chastity is not
what we should have expected had the book
merely been a mystification. It might have been
supposed that, had this been the case, the writer
would have selected for description a type of
girdle to which he would be accustomed from
the records already published. But Mlle. Lajon's
girdle has little in common with the specimens
we have described and which are on view in the
museums. It resembles somewhat more the
Falster case specimen, and as such may have
been a piece of apparatus devised on the spot
and made locally to Berhle's order. However
that may be, we cannot say that the authenticity

of the Freydier Plaidoyer has been finally established. If the trial really took place it is quite possible that notices of the fact and of the part that Freydier played in it may eventually turn up in letters and memoirs of the period. I have not yet succeeded in tracing anything of importance, but I trust that others, better acquainted with the local literature of Gard than myself may be more fortunate in this respect.

The next case which claims our attention is the so-called Cazanova-Carré Case, which is of interest as the point in dispute did not arise over the practical application of a girdle of chastity but its use for purposes of fiction.

In 1881 there appeared in Paris a book published serially in weekly parts at ten centimes per issue. The work, which bore the title of *La Ceinture de Chasteté*, has as the name of the author " J. Cazanova ", a pseudonym, which obviously had been chosen by the writer to confuse the public mind and to persuade the more gullible that the book was the work of Casanova himself. Certain of the parts were accompanied by illustrations and the whole appeared under the auspices of the publishing house of Wormus.[1]

---

[1] Later modern editions have been published under the name of Casanova, thus further imposing upon the ill-informed. Those of the modern copies that I have examined bear upon the wrapper an illustration totally distinct from that of the original edition.

THE GIRDLE OF CHASTITY

From the present point of view the book is harmless enough. Even the authorities of the Bibliothèque Nationale, who place works in the "Enfer" section which do not even have to be consulted in the North Library in the British Museum (so innocent are they), place this book where it can be consulted without waiting weeks for permission from the Comité consultatif. It is a dull account of the amours of various persons, and the use of the girdle of chastity is merely an incident in an interminable series of events which cover over three hundred pages. The engraved frontispiece shows a woman standing with her back to the observer. She is naked above the hips and her skirt falls just below the buttocks. A man is half kneeling behind her and is adjusting a narrow band above the nates which is evidently that to which is secured a chastity plate in front.

The story tells how a young woman was married to a jealous husband by name de Roujan. On their wedding night he tells her of certain girdles of chastity with which he became acquainted during a pilgrimage to Jerusalem. He procured three or four of these belts and brought them back with him. One day, when his wife is under the influence of a narcotic he has her measured, and in due course he shows her a box in which are the girdles he has bought. He proceeds to fit one, and having done so, he locks it and removes the key.

The apparatus consisted essentially of a broad band of double silken material which enclosed a series of thin springs. In front this band extended from below the navel to the beginning of the thighs, which it encased like a pair of bathing drawers. It was supported around the hips by a band of the width of three fingers, which, passing above the buttocks, left these bare. Between the legs was a longitudinal opening in the material, and a thin edging of gold surrounded this orifice which was perforated by numbers of small holes from which emerged, under the slightest pressure on the springs, a number of needles which crossed one over the other in order to protect the opening.[1] In due course the lover appears : the insulted lady throws herself into his arms and at the same moment de Roujan appears, revolver in hand, on the threshold.

The illustration [2] which seems to have excited condemnation was that on the wrapper which we have already described, but it can hardly be said that it is in any way obscene and the objection to it is now not easy to understand.

[1] J. Cazanova, *op. cit.*, p. 15.
[2] Cf. the eighteenth century French engraving of the husband unlocking his wife's girdle reproduced in *Sittengeschichte des Intimen*, hrsg. v L. Schidrowitz (Wien [1926]), p. 47.

However some weeks after the appearance of a few of the numbers the law began to move, and on 10th January, 1884, the sixth chamber of the "Tribunal Correctionnel de la Seine" gave judgment against the publisher. He was accused of publishing, putting on sale and selling a book with designs both on the wrapper and in the text which were considered to awaken obscene ideas ; and also of allowing to be included in the text certain passages dealing with a girdle of chastity. The character of the illustrations were said not only to wound certain susceptibilities but also to accentuate the immoral nature of the book, which in addition was wrongly attributed to Casanova. The opinion of the court was therefore against the publisher and Wormus was sentenced to six days' imprisonment and a fine of five hundred francs.

Against this sentence Wormus appealed and his defence was undertaken by Carré, who, in an excellent speech, summed up the evidence against his client and showed that it was both unjust and unfair. He began by pointing out how difficult it was to judge of literary and artistic production, especially at a time when all around them they saw

> Ces placards éhontés, debaucheurs de passants
> Qui tuaient la pudeur dans les yeux des enfants.

On reading the book he found himself unable to discover even " l'ombre d'un délit ", and he has been much troubled by the severe sentence imposed upon his client. It was not to be imagined that Wormus was the publisher of pornographic and obscene works. He issued numbers of books of scientific value, and the author of the book in question was a literary man who wished to preserve his anonymity. But at the end of five weeks the book was seized and condemned under the law of 2nd August, 1882. As regards the engravings he found nothing in them which was worthy of condemnation. There was not even an uncovered bosom to be found, and masters like Watteau, Boucher, Baudouin and Greuze have done far worse things. The shops were full of nudities, and yet this book was the one to be seized and condemned. As to the text, Brantôme had dealt with girdles, and in the works of Maupassant, Musset, and Montesquieu could be found far worse passages than any in *La Ceinture de Chasteté*. Latin literature could be condemned, Carré continued, on the same grounds, and his speech was concluded by the quotation from Voltaire, " Je connais beaucoup de livres qui ont ennuyé ; je ne'en connais point qui ait fait de mal réel."

After Carré's address had finished the court

was obviously impressed. The appeal **was** granted and Wormus was discharged.[1]

It is not easy to understand why " Cazanova's " book was selected by the French authorities as one suitable for prosecution. The fact that it seems that in April, 1882, an actual case of this sort occurred in Spain can hardly have influenced them. In this instance a charge was brought before a judge, Maroto, in the little town of Buonavisita, Province of León. It appeared that a young woman had visited a hospital and had asked for assistance in getting rid of a certain piece of apparatus which she had had forced upon her by her lover, a medical man, who had procured it at Benevente in the north-east of the Province of Zamora. The girdle is described as a small device which was arranged around the middle of the body and between the inguinal regions.[2]

A similar case seems to have been dragged to light towards 1830 at Weimar, but I have not seen any details and am not aware if legal proceedings were instituted or not.[3] A more interesting instance related by Debay is said

[1] See *La Ceinture de Chasteté avec la Plaidoirie de M. E. Carré* (2 vols., Paris, 1886). The speech will also be found in the *Revue des grands procès contemporains*, 1887, v, 425–36.

[2] See *El Liberal*, 20th April, 1882, quoted by Caufeynon, *op. cit.*, pp. 97 ff.

[3] J. S. Ersch and J. G. Gruber, *op. cit.*, sect. 2 (1840), Th. 18, pp. 159–60.

to have occurred in France, and is published in the writer's *Hygiène et physiologie de mariage.* He says, by way of introduction, that in Italy, Spain, and Portugal women are sometimes accustomed to wear girdles of chastity. Indeed at one time he says that it became general in the larger cities, although in France it " ne prit que très faiblement ", for husbands are less jealous in that country and more philosophical, for they know that mechanical obstacles are of little value.

In the present instance, however, a girdle was used. It appears that a young woman married a man of advanced years, who moved in brilliant society and whom his wife accompanied to many social functions of importance. In the course of time the lady became the object of attention of a young man, who followed her everywhere, but to whose solicitation she did not respond. Her husband, however, suspected her of infidelity, and forced her to wear a chastity belt, which he locked and the key of which he retained. Thereupon the injured wife took an imprint of the lock, had a key made, and wrote to her suitor for an assignation. When he arrived she met him and presented him with the duplicate key telling him that up till then she had been faithful and virtuous, but since her husband on account of his atrocious jealousy had wished to make himself the guardian of her virtue she had resolved to yield it to another. Having done so she was filled with remorse.[1]

The only comment that can be made on this story is that made on such a jealous husband by René Hémard:

" Pauure ialoux, concierge infame,
  Diable obsedant toüioirs ta femme,
  C'est inutilement que tu fais tant de pas,
  Tu trauailles toy-mesme apres cocüage :
  On ne doit pas garder vne femme bien sage,
  Et l'on ne peut garder celle qui ne l'est pas." [2]

Another case which does not seem to have attracted the attention of the legal authorities of the day occurred, it seems, somewhere in Bohemia towards 1871. At any rate the story was told by the victim to Dr. Ladislav Šir, who published it in a medical journal.[3]

The case is of some interest, as it illustrates an Oriental form of female infibulation, and perhaps is scarcely relevant in an account of the chastity belt. I include it, however, as it

---

[1] A. Debay, *op. cit.*, pp. 21–2.
[2] R. Hémard, *Les restes de la Guerre d'Estampes* (Paris, 1880), p. 45. Cf. F. de Maynard, *Priapées* (Freetown [Bruxelles], 1864), p. 51.
[3] L. Šir, *Případy z praxe lékařské : novověký opasek na ohanbí* (Časopis lékařův českých, 15. dubna, 1871, x, 114. Cf. Tlusty, *Weiberverschluss* (Sexual-Probleme, 1910, Jahrg. vi, 69–70).

has not been published before in English and is hardly known in this country.

It appears that at the age of twenty-three a young woman married a locksmith. After some time had passed the husband forced his wife into a life of prostitution, acting as her *souteneur* and virtually living upon her earnings. This continued for a few years until the girl became too ill to continue her profession. On her recovery she refused to go back to her former mode of life and decided instead to enter some business. The news instantly aroused the worst suspicions in the heart of her husband. Believing that his wife would inevitably drift back to the old life but this time keep her earnings for herself, he determined to prevent this possibility by taking a drastic step. One day he seized her and declared that before he would permit her to go to business he would have to perform a certain operation. Thereupon he took a sharp pointed instrument and bored through one of the labia by means of it.[1] Through the orifice thus created he inserted a small metal band which he bent round and

---

[1] It is not clear from the narrative precisely what was perforated, but it would seem that it may have been the *labia minora*, which when drawn together by the padlock would offer a barrier to illicit intercourse. This was the case in an American report of a lock fitted to a German woman. (See H. L. Collyer in *Amer. Med.-Surg. Bulletin*, 15th December, 1894, vii, 1523, reported to G. M. Gould and W. L. Pyle, *Anomalies and Curiosities of Medicine*, Philadelphia, 1897, p 753.)

removed every day over a certain period.[1] The same operation was then performed upon the other labium and finally he made a small lock, and, driving the link through both holes, secured it with a key which he put in his pocket. Although the lock was quite light, weighing only about one and a half ounces, it was far from comfortable, and the young woman found it necessary to wear a silk bandage. After three weeks had elapsed she returned, got her husband to remove it, and again consented to have it replaced when she returned to her business. This continued for several years, and the practice was only finally discarded when her advancing years seemed to her husband a sufficient guarantee against illicit amours.[2]

---

[1] Cf. A. C. Celsus, *De Medicina* (Leipsic, 1859), lib. vii, cap. 25, sect. 3, p. 306.

[2] This story may be compared with that of the Leicester case of 1737 (see E. J. Dingwall, *op. cit.*, p. 59). A similar incident was reported by Dr. P. Soloviev in the Русскато Врача, 1906, No. 45, 1421, and reviewed by Rizat in the *Annales des maladies des organes génitaux-urinaires* for 1908, xxvi, (i), 555. It appears that in March, 1906, a young peasant, violently jealous in disposition, knocked his wife on the head, thereby stunning her, and then proceeded to pass two rings through her labia majora. In the following July a third ring was added and in October he joined all three rings with a copper fibula or padlock. Another case of actual infibulation was that reported in 1917 by N. K. Kallian-walla in the *Indian Medical Gazette*, Calcutta, lii, 284. Here silk ligatures were employed to secure the labia majora and another loop was inserted into the skin of the abdomen one inch below the navel. Such cases are often found in medical practice. In 1825 Legros states that he knew of a woman whose labia majora had been perforated for wearing a ring, and on one occasion a suspicious husband consulted him as to the best operation for ensuring the chastity of his wife. (F. Legros, in the *Gazette des Hôpitaux civils et militaires*, 1844, 2° sér.,

Another modern case which created a sensation at the time and in which the parties concerned came into conflict with the law was the famous Hufferte case which occurred in Bordeaux in 1892.

From contemporary and other records it seems that in the middle of March, 1892, the police of Bordeaux arrested one J. Hufferte, aged 40, who was employed in an important jam factory in the city. Hufferte was accused of having violated a young girl some four years previously, by name Anna B., who had been working under him at the same factory where he had his job. When Hufferte was arrested the child was only 17 years old, so at the time of the rape she could not have been more than 13.

The accusations, however, did not end there. The prisoner was also charged with having conspired with a woman named Lambeye, living at Rue des Morceux, 26, and with her assistance, enticed Anna away from her home and found for her a room in the same street

vi, 180.) Some have apparently believed that the passage concerning Count Eulalius of Clermont in the Ecclesiastical History of Gregory of Tours refers to the practice of infibulation : " *Sed concubinæ ejus instigante, ut quidam afferunt, invidia, maleficiis sensum ejus oppilaverunt,*" but there is no evidence for this, a magical process of some sort being more probably indicated. (See *Hist. eccles. Franc. lib. decem* (*Rec. d. Hist. d. Gaules et de la France* (Paris, 1739)), lib. x, 8, p. 367 d, and cf. P. Noury, *op. cit.*, p. 611).

at No. 40 where he got Lambeye to look after her and act as her guardian.

According to Anna's own statement the affair began in 1888, when she was engaged to work in the jam factory. One day, she declared, Hufferte had enticed her into a house in the Rue des Palanques and had there violated her. In order to prevent her from complaining he had threatened to have her dismissed from her employment if she spoke, and, terrified by the prospect of the possibility of losing her job, she consented to remain silent. Subsequently further intimacy took place, and finally Anna's grandmother, with whom she was then living, died. Hufferte thereupon found Anna another room in the Rue des Morceux, continued his relations with her and persuaded his accomplice, Lambeye, to look after her. It was about this period, it seems, that jealousy began to make itself felt. He kept a strict watch over Anna's movements and finally forced her to wear a kind of chastity belt which effectually prevented her from indulging her sexual desires with anyone but the man who had made her his mistress. While the affair was thus going on not a breath of suspicion seems to have reached the factory where the couple were still working. M. Stiévenin, the staff manager, declared that he was in no way mixed up with the business ;

and possibly all would have remained hidden, had not Anna, tired of her life and of Hufferte's jealousy, resolved to complain. One day she did not return to her room, and took refuge instead with a family of respectable antecedents to whom apparently she confided her trouble. Horrified at the tale she unfolded, they caused careful inquiries to be made. The result was that both Hufferte and Lambeye were arrested, and at the trial, which was for the most part held *in camera*, the facts were dragged to light. Hufferte was condemned to two years' imprisonment, but the woman Lambeye was acquitted.[1]

Almost ten years after the Hufferte trial in Bordeaux another case startled the legal world. The sculptor Ancilotti, a resident apparently of Rome, was found to have forced his wife Ondina Randone to wear a girdle of chastity, consisting of a kind of tight fitting and closely woven pair of drawers to which were attached steel rings at the appropriate parts, and which was secured by some form of locking device. This preposterous garment had obviously none of the advantages to the wearer afforded by the standard pattern of the girdle of chastity, and it was necessary to remove it twice a day, which the obliging husband consented to do.

[1] See *La Gironde*, mars, 1892; *Le Temps*, 15, 24 mars, 1892; Caufeynon, *op. cit.*, pp. 100 ff.

According to the records of the trial it appears that not only was Signora Ancilotti forced to wear the girdle when she was perfectly well but also during the latter months of pregnancy. A female witness, one Passalina, who was a friend of the unfortunate victim, not only described the form of the drawers with their iron rings, but also narrated the desperate straits to which the poor woman was subjected in the temporary absence of her jealous master. One day when the couple were travelling together to Turin, Signora Ancilotti complained to Passalina of the discomfort she was suffering owing to the presence of the " girdle " ; and the climax was reached when she became pregnant. One day when in this condition she had gone out to supper with a friend, Signora Adele Gaumier. During the course of the meal she found herself inconvenienced and had the humiliation of being forced to wait until she heard her husband whistling in the street, whereupon she went downstairs and returned with the key, explaining that it was the key to her chastity belt. Signora Gaumier assisted her to rid herself of the irksome contrivance, but, having fulfilled her need she again donned the belt and returned to the street to hand over the key to her husband !

In the end, however, the facts were exposed

114

and Ancilotti was arrested and brought to justice. In the course of the trial Professor Pieroni declared that Ancilotti himself had told him that he had made the belt with his own hands, and that he took also upon himself the task of undoing it twice a day, at noon and again at eight in the evening.[1] Although there seems to have been another case in Paris in 1899 [2] it does not appear to have excited the attention that the so-called Affaire Parat did in February, 1910. For on the eighteenth of that month Parisians awakened to a scandal which convulsed the capital for many weeks. *Le Petit Parisien* [3] appeared with an article entitled " L'Othello de la Rue Vaugirard " only to be followed by another next day called " Jean Parat : le pharmacien tortionnaire ". Similarly *Le Journal* discussed the same day the case of L'Othello de Vaugirard[4] ; and even the *Daily Telegraph* of London published an article on 19th February headed " A Wife in Chains ",[5] a title borrowed the Sunday following by the London *People*,[6] the same thing being printed in the London *News of the World* as " Clothed in Mail ".[7]

[1] See O. Kahn, *Weiberverschluss*, ii (Sexual-Probleme, 1910), Jahrg. vi, 71.
[2] M. Kemmerich, *Kultur-Kuriosa* (2 vols., München, 1924), vol. ii, p. 162.   [3] No. 12165, pp. 1, 3.
[4] Cf. issues for Fév. 20–5.   [5] *Op. cit.*, p. 9.
[6] *Op. cit.*, p. 6.   [7] *Op. cit.*, p. 5.

It would appear from the records that Jean Parat, an apothecary of 43 with a shop in the Rue de Vaugirard, had been suspected of cruelty to his young wife as early as 1908, but no action had then been taken. Later, however, suspicions were again aroused, it being said that when Parat left the house he chained his wife to a bed post. The Paris police began their investigations ; visited Parat's establishment, and there found his wife not only chained to the bed as had been reported, but wearing under her clothes an elaborate kind of corset made of chain mail and padlocked around the body, whilst her whole person was restrained by a perfect maze of chains and locks. She was instantly released from her bonds : Parat was arrested, tried, and sent to prison. When indicted with the crime the apothecary confessed it, declaring that he was animated by an intense jealousy which he tried to alleviate by taking these desperate measures to ensure the fidelity of his wife. Anyway, he said, as if to condone the offence, the chains were long enough for her to be able to play the piano. In *Le Rire* of 5th March Métivet contributed a cartoon of Parat dragging his wife after him. Beneath ran the legend, " V'là le moyen d'avoir une épouse bien ficilée et qui vous soit solidement attachée ".[1]

[1] *Op cit.*, p. 1.

We do not know how many Parisians took the
hint. At any rate the sale of girdles does not
seem to have increased after 1910. Lest my
readers may imagine that such cases are isolated
and that the use of these belts and apparatus
was restricted to maniacs who manufactured
them themselves, I may refer appropriately
here to two specimens of prospectus which seem
to have been issued in France probably somewhere between 1860 and 1900. The first of them
is said to have been published by a firm of
surgical instrument makers in Reims. It read :—

PLUS DE VIOLS
Appareil gardien de la fidélité des femmes
Avec armure et serrure simples . 120fr.
Avec armure et serrure simples
soignées et de luxe . . . . . . 180fr.
Avec armure et serrure simples en
argent, le tout très soigné . . . . 320fr.

On l'expedie, moyennant au bon sur la poste,
à l'ordre de M. Cambon, notaire et maire à
Cassagnes-Comtaux, par Rignac (Aveyron)
chargé de recevoir les fonds et d'en être garant.
Une semblable invention n'a pas besoin d'éloges.
Chacun sent les services qu'elle peut rendre.
Grâce à elle on pourra mettre les jeunes filles à
l'abri de ces malheurs qui les couvrent de honte
et plongent les familles dans le deuil. Le mari

117

quittera sa femme, sans crainte d'être outragé dans son honneur et dans ses affections. Bien des discussions, bien des turpitudes cesseront. Les pères seront sûrs d'être pères, et n'auront pas la terrible pensée que leurs enfants peuvent les enfants d'un autre, et il leur sera possible d'avoir sous la clef des choses plus précieuses que l'or. Dans un temps de désordre comme celui où nous vivons, où il y a tant d'époux dupes, tant de mères trompées, j'ai cru faire une bonne action et rendre service à la société en lui offrant une invention destinée à protéger les bonnes moeurs. Et il a fallu être bien sûr de son utilité pour l'annoncer et braver les plaisanteries qui l'entoureront.

On dira que l'entreprise est folle.

Mais quel est le plus fou, l'inventeur de la camisole de force ou ceux qui en ont besoin ?[1]

From the above it will be seen that the good M. Cambon supplied no less than three varieties of girdles, one kind being of silver, very neatly finished and costing only three hundred and twenty francs. As the prospectus says, the advantages are manifold. Not only will the purity of the virgin be maintained, but the fidelity of the wife exacted. " The husband will leave his wife without the fear that his

---

[1] See *Interm. des chercheurs*, etc., 1879, xii, pp. 496–7.

honour will be outraged and his affections estranged. Many discussions and shameful actions will cease. Fathers will be sure of their parenthood and will not harbour the terrible thought that their children may be the offspring of another, and it will be possible for them to keep under lock and key things more precious than gold." Indeed it would seem that the apparatus was well worth the money of the nineteenth century French husbands, who braved the jests which surrounded the use of such a device, for, as the folder asks, which is the bigger fool, the inventor of the " camisole de force " or he who has the use for it ?

History does not tell us whether M. Cambon had suffered the domestic troubles which the girdles were meant to alleviate. He must, at any rate, have been a brave man, for Cassagnes-Comtaux was not a large city : in about 1880 it boasted only some 1500 inhabitants. Besides dispatching ready-made girdles to those in need it was possible to obtain the apparatus to measure. One gentleman wrote and made inquiries on this score, receiving the following letter in reply.

Sir,—

In reply to your communication received this morning, I hasten to inform you that I can make the girdle for which you ask me. The measurement required is the circumference of the pelvis, this being taken a little high behind so that in front it passes just below the navel. The circumference of the thighs is also required.

The cost of this piece of apparatus is 100 francs . . .

Or again in another letter the firm describes a girdle which has been inquired for by a customer. It reads :—

Sir,—

Your esteemed letter of the 18th instant to hand. I can make the object you wish. It is made of metal, being of silver-gilt on the inside in order to avoid oxidation. The apparatus can be made in the way you desire affording protection both in front and behind. But I must inform you that there is a drawback to the latter, namely that in order to go to stool it is necessary to remove the apparatus, which otherwise need not be done, for urination is accomplished with the apparatus in position. It closes with a safety lock.

The prices are : For the apparatus with frontal plate only, 300fr. For the apparatus with double plate, 500 fr. The measurements to be taken are :—The circumference of the body taken below the pubis as shown by the

dotted line [i.e. in the diagram attached to the
letter] and secondly the width of the pubis as
indicated by the arrow [1] . . .

The second prospectus is one which is thought
to have been issued about 1885. It reads :—

PLUS DE VIOLS !
De l'édozone ou ceinture de pudeur.
D'autres appareils
gardiens de la fidélité de la femme et de
l'homme à différentes époques et dans
divers pays.
Manière d'en construire
secretèment et facilement.
Extraits de nombreuses lettres à ce sujet.[2]

From the above, the original of which I have
not seen, and which has been quoted without
giving the name of the firm or of any of the
details, it would appear that apparatus for men
was also being made by French instrument
makers of the period. It is probable that these
devices were of a similar nature to the pieces of
apparatus for prevention of masturbation among
boys which had a wide vogue in France at one
time, and were much recommended in different
quarters. The famous Jalado-Lafond constructed a number in the early years of the

---

[1] See E. Fuchs, *Ill. Sittengeschichte*, etc., vol. vi, pp. 131–2.
[2] *Interm. des chercheurs*, etc., 1900, xli, p. 919.

nineteenth century and he claims to have had
the experience of twenty years behind him. He
advised the use of a wide belt or corset made of
some strong woven material. To this was
attached a metal box or container (to hold the
external genitals), of which the outer tube was
perforated at the end, the sides being drilled for
purposes of ventilation. The whole was secured
around the body by means of locks. As we shall
see John Moodie revived it in a new and
ingenious manner in the middle of the nineteenth century.[1]

Even in Germany such ideas were not unknown. As late as 16th March, 1903, Frau Emilie
Schäfer, of 26 Rigaerstrasse, Berlin, applied for
a patent (Sch. 16096 : Gebrauchmuster 30.
d. 204538) for a " Verschliessbares Schutznetz
für Frauen gegen eheliche Untreue " (Girdle
with lock and key as a protection against
conjugal infidelity).[2]

Similar contrivances must have been devised
and used in various parts of Europe and the
United States for many years. I am informed

[1] G. Jalado-Lafond, *Considérations sur les bandages herniaires* . . .
(Paris, 1818), pp. 88 ff. A part was subsequently published containing
an account of the girdle reprinted from the book. For drawing of
apparatus see *Handbuch der Sexualwissenschaften* . . . hrsg. v. A. Moll;
2 Aufl. (Leipzig, 1921), p. 627.
[2] See *Vierte Beilage zum Deutschen Reichsanzeiger und Königlich
Preussischen Staatsanzeiger*, Montag, den 3 August, 1903, No. 180, p. 2 ;
P. B[lock], in the *Berliner Tageblatt*, 22 Feb., 1910, Jahrg. 39, No. 96 ;
Bilder-Lexikon der Erotik (Wien, Leipzig, 1928–30), vol. i, p. 527.

that inquiries for girdles of chastity are still occasionally made to-day of surgical instrument makers in London, and doubtless such are sometimes supplied. But they are, I think, no longer openly advocated. The last book published in Great Britain which advised their use was, if I mistake not, that published in Edinburgh in 1848 entitled *A medical treatise ; with principles and observations to preserve chastity and morality.* The work is so curious that the author deserves a chapter to himself.

CHAPTER IV

JOHN MOODIE, M.D., AND SURGEON.

Towards the middle of the nineteenth century there lived somewhere apparently in Scotland and probably in Edinburgh a certain John Moodie, who was accustomed to describe himself on the title-pages of his books as "M.D., and Surgeon".

There is a certain mystery about John Moodie. His name eludes our search in the records of the period, and his printers are but a name in the old Edinburgh street where they were formerly carrying on their business. We do not know, it seems, whether John Moodie graduated at Edinburgh or not. A "Joannes Moodie, Scotus," certainly graduated at the University in 1839 with a thesis on dysentery, but the thesis was apparently never printed and the MS. is not in the University Library. Medical scholars in Edinburgh have long forgotten this strange character, and inquiries at old-established surgical instrument makers have not led me to discover any Edinburgh firm which made the girdles of chastity that Moodie recommended. Perhaps John Moodie was just a quack doctor and in addition it would seem from a perusal of his books that he was just a little queer.

124

JOHN MOODIE, M.D.

But however eccentric Moodie may have been, it would be entirely wrong to suppose that he was mad, or even that he was a violent, stupid or pig-headed crank. He was nothing of the sort. Some of his remarks are noteworthy for their sense and grip of realities,[1] and it is only now and then that indications crop up which show that Moodie's mind had odd kinks in it which showed themselves in curious and unexpected ways. For instance in 1850 appeared a book by him entitled "*A new strict entail of £1500 a-year or less, for one hundred years. . .*" At the end, on the back of page 69, occurs a paragraph headed :—

"Extract "—which states that unchaste women or those who masturbate will be barren and ends by asking the question "What are the bad practices of Boarding School Misses ? "

Now this nonsense is quite unlike the general material which Moodie produced, and moreover is wholly out of place at the end of a book on a new strict entail. However, there it is, and it seems probable that the paragraph may have been inspired by memories of a former publication, now long forgotten, although copies still linger neglected on the shelves of our great

[1] Cf. his remarks on the morality of mining girls and of scanty dresses for women in his *Principles and Observations on many and various Subjects for the Health of Nations and Individuals* (Edinburgh, 1848), pt. i, p. 33.

libraries. This amazing book was published in Edinburgh in 1848 and is that mentioned at the conclusion of the last chapter.

It consists essentially of three main parts. One section is concerned with the asserted widespread use of the godemiché amongst Scottish ladies of the period, which statement can be linked up with the second part which comprises a detailed account of the need and the method of making satisfactory girdles of chastity for Scottish maidens. The third section is concerned mainly with an account of an ingenious piece of apparatus for preventing masturbation amongst boys, which can be compared with that we have previously described from Jalado-Lafond.

The female girdle of chastity seems to have been devised by Moodie mainly as a preventive of masturbation amongst girls, which, according to him, was terribly prevalent and was carried out not only digitally but also with the help of the godemiché. These objects, he says, were constantly in use, and indeed it was more common for married women to have them than to be without. Moreover mothers used to teach their girls how to use them, and altogether the moral condition of Scottish womanhood was, according to our author, not desirable.

The Moodie girdle of chastity consisted of a

cushion made out of rubber or some other soft material and suitably covered with silk, linen or soft leather. This cushion or pad formed the base into which was fixed a kind of grating, and this part of the apparatus rested upon the vulva, the pad being large enough to press upon the mons veneris. The lower part of the pad rested upon the perineum, being curved so as to fit the parts to be enclosed. The bars of the grating were to be made of ivory or bone and were so arranged in the pad that when in position they pressed up against the labia majora opposite the vagina. The whole apparatus was affixed by means of belts to a pair of tight-fitting drawers and secured by a padlock, a secret flap being made so as to close over the key hole. Not only was this device, declared Moodie, an effectual remedy against mastur-bation, but also as a means of avoiding seduction it had a " high and essential importance ".

As far as I have been able to discover the book was treated with silence by the medical world. Reviews do not seem to have been common, and probably it was thought that ignoring the book was the most effective reply to the calumnies therein contained and the abominable insinuations against the purity and morality of the women of Scotland. How far the apparatus was ever used is hard to say.

I have never seen an example myself, but possibly there may be examples still existing. Moreover the truth of Moodie's statements regarding the widespread use of the godemiché in Scotland ought to be examined, and I hope to return to these charges in another volume. However that may be, the book is unique, and, whatever value it may have viewed as an historical document, it is a remarkable addition to the scanty literature dealing with the use and advantages of the girdle of chastity.

CHAPTER V

THE GIRDLE OF CHASTITY IN LITERATURE

From a consideration of the preceding chapters it will be clearly seen what a field for wit and satire the use of the girdle of chastity offered to the writers of romance and poetry, legend and facetiæ. From the fifteenth to the twentieth century writers have now and then chosen to use this subject either as their central theme or at least as an item in the general course of their narrative.

In order to give the general reader some idea of the kinds of literary works which contain notices of girdles of chastity I propose to make what I hope to be a fairly representative selection of them and summarize their contents so far as these relate to the present discussion.

Since the chastity belt probably made its first appearance in ordinary use among the Italians of the period of the Renaissance or perhaps somewhat later, we may well begin our brief survey with an Italian author, Girolamo Morlini, who flourished in the first quarter of the sixteenth century. He is well known as the author of a volume of short stories and anecdotes, some of which are very amusing and throw a vivid light on the customs and foibles of his day. Although many are not what would be considered in the best of taste according to modern notions, yet they must have been much enjoyed at the time when they were written, and even now the story of the young man who was caught by an outraged husband and of the punishment meted out to him cannot fail to take the fancy of all but the most squeamish.

The tale relates how a married woman became enamoured of a young man who was exceedingly fair to look upon. So desirous indeed became the lady that she did all in her power to attract the attention of the youth and finally succeeded in seducing him. A meeting was arranged and everything went off satisfactorily. Mutual enjoyment and desire paved the way for a night of pleasure, " sicque supra illum sensim residens ac crebre subsilens, lubricisque gestibus mobilem spinam quatiens, pendulae veneris fructu illum satiavit ". But unfortunately time passed and before they had parted the door opened and the injured husband appeared. We need not repeat here what punishment he gave to the young lover of his faithless wife. Suffice to say that with her he took gentler although perhaps more drastic steps. He procured and fitted to her a girdle of chastity, or as the tale puts it, " pone uxoris foraminata vulva cardine reclusa," saying that now he happily could go about in safety.

In another story Morlini relates how a nun, unable to remain continent, invited a noble from Milan to share her couch, and the latter, accepting her proposal, and being of an absent-minded disposition, appeared next day, to the delight of all who saw him, in the habit of a monk, for that holy man had left it in the room of the nun on the occasion of a previous visit. This incident made a deep impression, and the conduct of the nun alarmed many when they thought of the possible faithlessness of their wives. At any rate they took steps to prevent any such disastrous accidents. " Et ab inde in antea nobiles Mediolanenses eorum mulieribus aureas argenteasque bracas supra umbilicum clave reclusas affabre fecerunt : relicta rimula meiendi atque excernendi foramine, illas liberas atque emancipatas accedere patiuntur." [And from that time the nobles of Milan constructed ingeniously made drawers of gold and silver for their wives which were closed above the navel by means of a key. A slit was left for the purposes of making water and an opening for defæcation and so the women were allowed to go free and independent.][1]

---

[1] G. Morlini, *Novellæ, fabulæ, comoedia* (Ed. 3, Lut. Parisiorum, 1855), Nov. xxxi, pp. 65–8 ; Nov. lxii, p. 115. Similarly Aretino, in the *Ragionamenti*, mentions the case of a woman who wore an iron girdle around her loins (*The Ragionamenti* (6 vols., Paris, 1889), vol. ii, p. 14).

From Italy we pass to France. And at the outset let me finally dismiss and bury a story which has been circulated for some years and which has, unfortunately, found a place in the new *Bilder-Lexikon der Erotik* now in course of publication. In the article on the *Keuschheitsgürtel* (Girdle of Chastity) in that work (vol. i, pp. 527, etc.) there is a statement that the chastity belt was mentioned by the poet Clément Marot. As far as I can trace it this story originated in a statement and long quotation by Eduard Fuchs on pp. 144–8 of the second volume of his *Illustrierte Sittengeschichte*.[1] In this place he repeats a story which need not detain us here and which he states occurs in the introduction to Marot's epigrams. For reference he gives the edition of the epigrams translated into German by Margarete Beutler-[Freksa], and edited by her husband. I have not yet been able to see a copy of this work, and I owe a debt of gratitude to my friend, Dr. Kurt Tautz, of the Prussian State Library, for discovering the address of Mrs. Freksa and for obtaining the facts. There is no copy of the edition in the State Library in Berlin and I do not know of any library where it can be consulted.[2]

---

[1] The Ergänzungsband to vol. i, Renaissance.

[2] C. Marot, *Epigramme. Übersetz. von M. Beutler*, hrsg. F. Freksa (München, 1908).

The introduction to Marot's epigrams, quoted by Fuchs as by Marot and apparently copied from him into the *Bilder-Lexicon*, is not by Marot but by the editor of the Beutler translation, or in other words by Mr. Fridrich Freksa. Thus, as far as I know, there is no mention in Marot's epigrams of the use of the girdle of chastity, or if there be, I have overlooked it and would be grateful for the correct reference.

As might be expected the girdle of chastity is not passed over silently in the works of Rabelais. In *Pantagruel*,[1] Panurge, when talking to Trouillogan, speaks of clapping a Bergamasco lock upon his wife, where reference is obviously being made to the application of a chastity belt which seems to have been associated with the town of Bergamo in Lombardy.

Whilst Rabelais was writing in France Sir David Lyndsay was composing some of his poems in Scotland. One would hardly expect to find any mention of girdles of chastity in Scottish poetry, but there is such a reference in the " Plocamatioun [Proclamatioun] of the Play, made be Dauid Lynſayis, of the Month, Knicht ", which is preserved in the Bannatyne Manuscript.

Various characters are introduced and at one

---

[1] F. Rabelais, *Pantagruel*, iii, 36.

point an old man enters leading his wife in a dance. He says :—

> " Beſſy, my hairt, I mon ly doun and ſleip,
> And in myne arme ſe quyetly thow creip ;
> Beſſy, my hairt, firſt lat me lok thy c—
> Syne lat me keip the key as I was wount."

His wife replies,

> " My gud huſband, lock it evin as ye pleiſs,
> I pray God ſend yow grit honor and eiſs."

Thereupon the old man locks his wife up, and, putting the key under his head, falls asleep. Various lovers then approach the fair Bessy in order to court her, but one only is favoured, although he has but few worldy possessions and only one attraction which in sooth is the best that ever was seen. Bessy welcomes him warmly, saying :

> " Now welcome to me aboif thame aw.
> Was nevir wyf ſa ſtraitly rokkit [secured],
> Se ye not how my c— is lokkit."

Her lover is disgusted and says,

> " Thinkis he nocht ſchame, that brybor
> [beggarly chap] blunt,
> To put ane lok vpoun your c— ? "

Bessy at a loss to know what to do suggests

134

stealing the key. Her lover does so without awakening the old man and Bessy then says,

> " Na, than lat ws ga play our fill."

They retire to a quiet spot, and after a time the old man comes along crying out for Bessy and saying,

> " My bony Beſſy, quhair art thow now ? "

He laments his misfortune on account of the disappearance of the key which he thinks has been lost, for it means that in all probability the lock will have to be forced and broken. Bessy then appears and asks what is the matter and what is it that he wants, and at the same time, by a skilful manoeuvre, the key is slipped back into its former position. The old man demands the key to the lock, but Bessy with a great show of astonishment replies,

> " Ye reve, gudman, be Goddis breid,
> I ſaw yow lay it vndir your heid."

The jealous old man then again hunts for the key and finds it, at which he becomes very pleased and praises his good little wifé in these terms,

> " I trow thair be no man in Fyffe,
> That evir had ſa gude ane wyfe ",

upon which the story of Bessy's girdle of chastity
is brought to a close.[1]

It was not long before the use of the girdle
became the subject of coarse burlesque and
extravagant farce. The various kinds of girdles
were becoming better known, as we can see from
the comedy *La Rome Ridicule*, which set the
fashion for works of this type. Its author,
Marc A. de Gérard, Sieur de Saint Amant, was
born almost at the end of the sixteenth century
and left behind him some poetry of merit. In
the piece, *La Rome Ridicule*, we read

> D'un Brayer que martel-en-teste
> De ses propres mains a forgés,
> Leurs femmes ont le bas chargé
> De peur qu'il ne fasse la Beste :
> Au moins on sçait qu'en la pluspart
> Leurs maris usant de cet art,
> Tant d'âpre soupçon les devore
> Mais ce fer a deux fins servant,
> Les fait voir plus jaloux encore
> Du derrière, que du devant,[2]

---

[1] See *The Bannatyne Manuscript*. Compiled by George Bannatyne,
1568. (Hunterian Club) (4 vols., Glasgow, 1896 [1873–1901]), vol. iii,
pp. 469–72. A new edition of the Bannatyne Manuscript is now being
issued under the auspices of the Scottish Text Society. The above
extracts appear in vol. iii, pp. 94–9 of this edition.

[2] M. A. de Gérard, Sieur de Saint Amant, *La Rome Ridicule* : *caprice*
(Paris, 1661), lxxxviii, p. 32. The word *brayer* is not the usual one for
ceinture de chasteté, but has another meaning which we cannot discuss
here. *Martel-en-teste* is here a proper name ; we should say " Mr.
Jealous " or " the jealous one ".

which does not reflect too highly on the morality
of those to whom it refers !

A few years after the appearance of *La Rome
Ridicule* the play, *L'Amour Sentinelle, ou le
Cadenas forcé,*[1] was published, the authorship
being attributed to D. C. de Nanteuil, but a fuller
treatment of the same theme is to be found in
the amusing volume of anecdotes called *Roger
Bontemps en belle humeur,* at the end of which
in the edition of 1670 will be found a supple-
mentary section entitled *Les heureuses advantures d'amour.* The sixteenth adventure
describes a case in which a girdle of chastity was
employed, and the narrator tells the tale in the
form of a story, which, he says, was told to him
by a young man to whom in turn it was related
by a citizen of Arles in Provence.

It was said that once upon a time a lady was
living in the town of Arles, but that it would be
wise to withhold her name since it was not
desirable that the circumstances should be
widely known, although the details were common
property at the time when the incident occurred.
At that time there was living in the town a
certain honest citizen who had but one serious
flaw in his character, namely that he was of an
extremely jealous disposition, although his wife
had never given him the slightest reason to

[1] *L'Amour Sentinelle, ou le Cadenas forcé* (La Haye, 1669).

doubt her fidelity. One day he found himself
compelled to undertake a somewhat long
journey, and, his head filled with imaginary
fears, he thought that there could be no better
means of allaying them than by treating his
wife after the manner of certain Italians and
presenting her with a lock, which jealous Italian
husbands are sometimes accustomed to bestow
upon their loved ones. This piece of apparatus
was a delicately made girdle of steel which
surrounded the loins and to which was attached
another steel strip which passed between the
legs of the wearer, and which, joining the first
band at the back of the body, was secured there
by a lock. The effect of this vertical band was
that it closed two avenues to pleasure without
depriving the wearer of the ability to fulfil the
natural functions. This worthy citizen of Arles,
then, had the belt made to his order and one day
presented it to her whom he so unreasonably
suspected. Just as he was going to depart he
called his innocent wife to him and fitted her
with what had to that time never been heard of
in France, after which he went away believing
that his plans would prove successful.

When he had left, his wife, firmly locked up
and very angry at seeing herself so badly treated,
resolved to avenge the insult, and fit to her
husband's head those appendages he thought

that he already possessed, or at heart feared that he might soon have.[1] The resolution made, the difficulty was to put it into practical execution. Several nights passed in deep thought as to the best way of carrying out the project, when suddenly she bethought herself of an honest man in the neighbourhood, who had formerly courted her, but whom she had always repulsed for the sake of her virtue and of her fair name.

So it happened that one day at church she greeted him very humbly as was not her usual custom, and this change in her demeanour gave him food for thought as to the meaning of this mark of favour, and at the same time caused him not to hesitate for an instant before greeting her and presenting her with his respects.

Later on when an opportunity occurred she made so bold as to call to him when she was alone and suggest a talk. She told him that the reason why she had not yielded in the past was owing to her determination to resist the flames of love, but that now she felt herself unable longer to resist and would abandon herself to him if he still so willed it. She went on to explain that when she had married she

---

[1] Cf. *Facetiae facetiarum, hoc est, Joco-seriorum fasciculus novus* . . . (Pathopoli, 1647), p. 466.

had believed herself to have a husband, but discovered too late that he was a tyrant who desired to hold both her body and her soul in subjection. Such a position was intolerable, and should her present companion liberate her she was his. Not fully understanding the drift of his companion's remarks, the man demanded an explanation, whereupon the lady, throwing aside all reserve, showed him the apparatus which encircled her. Horrified by the sight, he declared that it would be necessary for a locksmith to be summoned in order to break it, but to this the lady would not consent. It was better in her view to construct a duplicate key, which was accordingly done, thus permitting both to enjoy each other and " à faire des images au naturel ". That is the way love rewards the constancy of lovers and the fidelity of hearts.[1]

It was perhaps about the same time that the above was being composed that men were reading that very notorious book the *Satyra Sotadica—the Dialogues of Luisa Sigœa*—which has the reputation of being one of the most obscene books ever written. The author is generally believed to have been Nicolas Chorier and the first edition may have been published

---

[1] *Roger Bontemps en belle humeur* (Cologne, 1670), pp. 468–72. The authorship of de Roquelaure seems to be doubtful.

towards 1680.[1] Chorier himself was born towards the beginning of the seventeenth century and died about 1692, and with the exception of the notorious dialogues his work is largely forgotten.

Amidst the mass of material dealt with in this book occurs a passage which is worthy of quotation since it deals with the girdle of chastity as it was then known. Tullia and Octavia are conversing about Julia and Jocondo and Octavia asks a question about the girdle of chastity which she has heard being mentioned.

Oct. "Audivi de cingulo pudicitiae, cum Julia, ante hos dies, nescio quid sermonis esse matri meae. Quae vero hujus cinguli ratio esse possit, quae pudicas reddat me latet." [I have heard recently I know not what conversation between Julia and my mother about this girdle of chastity. But indeed I do not understand the working of this girdle which makes women chaste.]

Tullia then proceeds to explain.

Tullia. "Disces. Postridie, cum surgeret Julia accessit Jocondus. Zonam illam, testibus amotis, explicat. Illa ridens:—'Quid hoc

<hr />

[1] *Aloisiæ Sigeæ Toletanæ satyra sotadica de arcanis amoris et veneris* : *Aloysia hispanice scripsit* : *latinitate donavit J. Meursius, V.C.* (Grenoble, pr., c. 1680).

sibi vult,' inquit, 'in quo aurum lucere video, quod affers ? ' —'Hoc te nunc cingi juvat,' ait ille, 'pudicitiae cingulo, et muniri adversus maternam labem. Cingulum pudicitiae vocant; hoc ante te plures annos Sempronia gessit, hear mea, et tu geres; ita egregiam sibi adepta est famam, quam etiam spero te tibi comparaturam.' Cataracta aurea quatuor pendet catenulis chalybeis, villoso sericeo panno indutis, quae cum cingulo eadem arte committuntur ejusdem metalli. Duae ab altero latere, duae itidem ab altero, cataractam a tergo et a fronte sustinent in eam immissae. Retro supra lumbos cingulum connectitur sera, cui tenuissima est clavis accommodata. Cataracta alta sex digitos plus minus, lata tres, sic a perinaeo pertingit ad summae exterioris rimae oram, et id spatium omne quod intercedit, utrumque inter femur tegit, infimumque uterum. Tribus radiis distincta apertis exitum lotio praebet, aditum vel summis digitis negat. Sic velut thorace adversus extraneas mentulas illa pars munitur, cujus usum, cum vult, facilem habet cui Hymenaei lege adjudicatus est."

[You shall understand it. The following day, when Julia got up, Jocondo approached her. With nobody present as a witness he

142

displays this girdle. Laughingly Julia says to him, " What is this which you are bringing and which I see all shining with gold ? " " You must now gird yourself with this ", says he, " it is a girdle of chastity, and you must be protected against the risk of motherhood. They call it a girdle of chastity ; my mistress Sempronia wore it for many years before you and you shall wear it ; thus was her fair fame acquired and I trust that yours may be comparable ". The grille of gold hangs from four little steel chains, encased in rough silken cloth which are joined in the same way to a belt of similar metal. The grille is supported both in front and behind by these four chains, two on the one side and likewise two on the other. Above the loins the belt is linked together by a fastener for which a very small key is adapted. The grille is about 6 inches high and 3 broad, thus extending from the perineum to the upper margin of the external lips, and covers the whole of that region which extends from between the thighs to the lower part of the belly. As the grille is fitted with three open bars it permits the passage of the urine, but prevents access even to the tips of the fingers. Thus as by a cuirass the part is defended against strange visitors, and he to whom the law of Hymen has granted it has an easy access when he wishes.[1]]

From the above account it will be seen that the girdle as described by Chorier is of a very simple variety, being merely a grille which is pressed up against the vulva and supported in position by four chains which are united to a hip belt passing round the body. It is totally different from the example credited to Carrara, where we have heavy perforated metal plates of which the holes are surrounded with rows of sharp teeth.

A few years after the appearance of the *Satyra Sotadica* there was published in Cologne (if we can trust the imprint) a little volume entitled *L'Amour en fureur, ou les excès de la jalousie italienne*. This work had a great success, for editions are known dating from 1690, 1696, 1698, 1710, 1715, and 1742. It deals almost exclusively with the adventures of a lady who was forced to wear a girdle of chastity, and in many respects it bears a strong resemblance to a tale by Antonio Cornazzano which is included in his book of *Proverbia* and is entitled "*Perche si dice. A buono intenditore poche parole*".[2]

The later story revolves around the jealousy

---

[1] *Aloisiæ Sigeæ Toletanæ Satyra Sotadica . . .* (Parisiis, 1885), pp. 116–17.
[2] A. Cornazzano, *Proverbia* (Vinegia, 1555), Prov. iii.

of a certain Fabricius, who tortured by suspicions regarding the fidelity of his wife, Virginie, resolves to fit her with a certain mysterious belt of which the use is well known in Italy but is not so common in other nations who dwell in a more temperate climate. The apparatus consisted essentially of a small grille to which were attached four little chains of steel, two of which supported the grille in front, and two behind. The ends of the chains were attached above the loins to a strong padlock controlled by springs, the secret of which was known only to the maker and the owner.

Having had the apparatus made, Fabricius resolved to fit it, and so one morning when his wife got out of bed, he sent the maids away and presented her with it. Virginie takes it but does not understand its use, and, when it is explained to her, refuses to wear it. Fabricius, however, informs her that he could produce many examples of its use, and finally Virginie consents to try it on. Her husband thereupon shows her how it is to be worn and exhibits with pride the glittering grille of gold with its decoration of inlaid work. Finally he fits it in position, locks it and removes the key, whilst even Virginie is obliged to laugh at the comical figure she cuts when wearing it. For some days she finds it rather uncomfortable, but her husband is delighted and allows her a liberty which she has not enjoyed for many a long day. The domestic calm, however, was soon to be followed by a storm. One day Virginie is caught flirting : Fabricius is furious, but is finally mollified when Virginie promises faithfully to be good and not to offend again.

Among the servants of the household there was a certain young Roman named Alessio, whom Fabricius had specially chosen to be one of the personal staff to wait upon Virginie. He is described as being a handsome and gallant young man, and in person he unfortunately reminded Virginie of the man whom she had loved before she had married her present husband. Up to that time Fabricius had not in the least suspected Alessio, but now his doubts were aroused and an incident of the most disastrous character led to a terrible scene. During a dance Virginie suddenly felt that part of her girdle had given way or had become detached, and in an agony of embarrassment beat a hasty retreat in order to investigate what had actually happened. Alessio, much intrigued by the sudden exit of his mistress, followed her and discovered the cause of the contretemps by peeping through a crack in the door. After having rearranged the girdle Virginie returned to the salon, and at dinner

146

by chance found herself for a short time alone with Alessio. Emboldened by what had occurred he suggested an affair but was immediately repelled by Virginie. Fabricius then began to suspect that all was not well, and when they retire he discovered that the girdle had been broken. Maddened with rage and jealousy he refused to believe Virginie's story of how it had occurred, and his intolerable behaviour led to a scene which ended by Virginie leaving him and passing the remainder of the night in a separate room. Next morning Fabricius met Virginie and expounded to her a new plan to meet the situation. All the servants are to be dismissed and an entirely fresh staff is to be engaged. Virginie agreed and Alessio is the first to be bundled out of the house by Fabricius, who thereupon proceeded to engage a staff of coloured servants and assigns to Virginie the ugliest of them all, a man named Ismaël. But even then his suspicions were not wholly lulled. He fitted Virginie with a more substantial girdle, and after some time had passed she became pregnant by her husband. A surprise, however, awaited them both. To their horror the baby, when born, resembled Ismaël, a result due, after the manner of the beliefs of the time, to pre-natal influences. But Fabricius will have none of this

147

theory when applied to his wife. In spite of the child dying soon after, Fabricius resolved to have no more trouble with Virginie and ordered some of his servants to drown her. She was seized and carried off, but the servants became softened towards her and finally allowed her to escape to a strange country on the condition that she never returned.

After a number of exciting adventures Virginie met her old flame, Camille, and filled with joy abandoned herself to him. Enchanted at meeting his lover after so long a separation, Camille took Virginie away with him, but on the first night together he discovered the girdle still in position, although Virginie had done all in her power to remove it.[1] Camille immediately began to struggle with it and tried a number of keys but only one out of the three locks yielded to his manipulations. He then proceeded to attack the girdle with his hands and tried to force the bars of the grille apart by main force, but his only reward was bleeding fingers and torn hands. He then rushed out of the room and ordered files to be brought, which he snatched from the hands of the servants and rushed back to his lover. Inflamed to frenzy

[1] Cf. the modern cartoon by J. Touchet, "*Die Demi-Vierge*," which shows a girl being undressed by a lover who finds her wearing a girdle of chastity (see *Sittengeschichte von Paris*: hrsg. v. L. Schidrowitz (Wien, Leipzig (1926)), p. 243.

by the sight of Virginie lying naked but for the girdle, he attacked it again with all his force till finally the chains succumbed to his furious onslaughts, the girdle fell off, and the tale ends as he gives to Virginie " des nouvelles preuves de sa vigueur et de son courage ".[1]

As has been said above, the first edition of *L'Amour en fureur* was published in 1684, but nearly thirty years previously another volume had been printed in Paris which might have been thought to contain a detailed account of girdles of chastity. This is, however, not the case. I refer to *L'Escole des Filles, ou la Philosophie des Dames*,[2] one of the most charming books of instruction in the *ars amandi* ever written, but unfortunately marred by a number of passages which have been emphasized by the prudish, and which have helped in gaining for the book the reputation of being the most obscene work in the French language for the time in which it was written. Even the author is unknown, and, as far as I am aware, not a single copy of the first edition has survived.

---

[1] *L'Amour en fureur, ou les excès de la jalousie italienne* (La Haye, 1742), pp. 27–130. The Neuchâtel edition of 1698 and also I think that of 1706 had frontispieces depicting a scene in which the girdle plays a part. Virginie has just locked the girdle and is handing the key over to Fabricius, who is standing at the foot of the bed before apparently going out, for his hat is on his head and his sword at his side. (For a reproduction see *Handbuch der Sexualwissenschaften* . . . hrsg. v. A. Moll ; 2. Aufl. (Leipzig, 1921), p. 236.

[2] *L'Escole des Filles*, etc. (Fribourg, 1668).

It has been variously attributed to Mililot, Helot, who was the son of an officer in the Cent Suisses of the King, or to Milot by Patin, who in a letter dated 26th July, 1655, described seeing his effigy hung on a gibbet by the Parisian mob for having written an infamous book based on Aretino.[1]

It is true that on its appearance the book was burnt and the author fled the city, his effigy being publicly hung upon the gallows.

The book itself is a detailed account of the amorous adventures of two girls and the instruction of one of them by her more experienced friend. There is, as I have said, no mention of a girdle of chastity, although the account of other pieces of apparatus for use in the erotic life are detailed and of great interest when one considers the date at which the book was composed.[2]

[1] See F. Charpentier, *Carpenteriana, ou recueil de pensées, bon mots de Charpentier* (Paris, 1724), p. 80; G. Patin, *Nouvelles lettres, tirées du cabinet de Mr. C. Spon* . . . (2 vols., Amsterdam, 1718), vol. ii, p. 123. I do not think that *L'Escole des Filles* is based upon *La Puttana errante* which was wrongly ascribed to Aretino, although appearing in the 1660 (Cosmopoli) edition of the *Cappricciosi e piaceuoli Ragionamenti*. The former work is far more spirited and well informed. It was reprinted in 1865 and issued under the auspices of Poulet-Malassis (see P. Dufay, *Poulet-Malassis à Bruxelles* (Mercure de France, 15 Nov. 1928, No. 730, 39e an., ccviii, 38–83). An English edition with critical and explanatory notes has not yet appeared, and it is remarkable that Ashbee in his three great works never analyzed *L'Escole des Filles*.

[2] Cf. for example the early form of condom described on p. 155 and also the elaborate merkin on p. 153. Perhaps they are better to-day. T. Petermann saw in an English rubber catalogue an advertisement of a perfect " femme de chambre " priced at £20 ! (*Ztschr. f. Sexualwissenschaft*, Leipzig, 1908, i, 294; cf. M. Hirschfeld, *Geschlechtskunde* (Stuttgart, 1926–9), vol. i, p. 266.

As the years went on the number of books in which the girdle of chastity figured as an essential item in the narrative remained about the same. The subject never assumed a very wide popularity, for the material offered only a limited field for literary exploitation and what could be said had for the most part been said before.

One of the most amusing satires on the use of the chastity belt is that to be found within the covers of that rare little book of doubtful authorship, *Satyres sur les femmes bourgeoises qui se font Madame*, which seems to have been issued in Paris about 1713, and bears an Epître signed "Le Chevalier D***," who is said by the authorities at the British Museum to be de Nisard, but who, as Brunet points out, was probably one d'Hennissart. It is the tale of

> Deux jeunes mariez de peu d'intelligence,
> N'ayant en leurs vertus aucune confiance,
> Pour s'asseurer tous deux de leur fidelité
> Convinrent d'un moyen assez bien inventé.

At that time there was a very clever and ingenious surgical instrument maker, by name Goubert, whose fame had travelled far and wide and who had contrived many an ingenious device and contraption,

> Qui sçavent contenir les mouvemens secrets,
> Malgré l'activité de nos feux indiscrets.

151

Monsieur Goubert was therefore sought out by the sceptical couple, who, when they found him said,

> "Faites-nous à chacun, Monsieur, une Ceinture
> Bien formante à la clef avec bonne serrure."

Thereupon Goubert took their measurements, and, having got to work, subsequently fitted them with the results of his labours which seemed so secure and ingeniously made that all distrust melted away. Later, however, the calm and domestic peace were ruffled. The wife believed that she had occasion to suspect that her husband cherished a secret attachment.

> Et qu'une fausse clef avoit pû sur cela
> Luy faire prendre ailleurs cette liberté-là.

Thereupon she went straight off to the worthy Monsieur Goubert and asked him to make her a duplicate key, but he firmly refused her request,

> "Si je vous accordois, luy dit-il en colère,
> Ce que vous demandoz, j'en aurois trop à faire,
> Les femmes que je sers en bon nombre à Paris,
> M'en vendroient demander pour tromper leurs maris,"

thus politely declining her suggestion and ending his speech by saying, doubtless with a shake of the head,

"Veuillez m'en dispenser, Madame, s'il vous plaît."

Thus baffled by her first attempt in her encounter with Goubert, the young wife then went in search of someone who would force the lock for her and finally a

Certain homme s'offrit ayant sçû son histoire,
Qui de la soulager se fit un point de gloire.

But her husband had been warned that his lock had been tampered with and he became very angry. Indeed the quarrel became so violent and the two became so heated that the end of the matter was that it was taken to the law courts and it was there that the learned judge gave orders that the girdles that the young people were wearing should be examined and that a report upon their condition should be made.

Le rapport de Goubert toûjours judicieux,
Fut qu'ils avoient enfin prévariqué tous deux,
Surquoy l'on prononça qu'aux fins de la
      Requête
Il seroit fait encore une nouvelle enquête,
Et par provision le jaloux decreté,
Par l'Huissier de service à l'instant arrêté.

On this discovery being made public the wife expressed her sorrow at what had occurred and she promised to answer for her husband upon the condition that her own liberty should be restored.

> Il consentit soudain étant alors vexé
> Et dans le même instant il se vit relaxé,
> Tous deux prirent l'effort malgré leur mariage,
> Et de leurs libertéz allerent faire usage.[1]

So the trouble ended happily and the uselessness of girdles was once again demonstrated. They were not often used by young people but were commonly restricted to the old and jealously inclined husband, like the one of whom Voltaire speaks in that odd document addressed to a lady against whom her husband had chosen to apply this precaution,

> " geôlier sexagénaire,
> Il a fermé le libre sanctuaire
> De vos appas ; et trompant nos désirs,
> Il tient la clef du séjour du plaisirs,"

for, he continues,

> " dans Venise et dans Rome,
> Il n'est pédant, bourgeois, ni gentilhomme,
> Qui, pour garder l'honneur de sa maison,
> De cadenas n'ait sa provision." [2]

[1] *Satyres sur les femmes bourgeoisies qui se font Madame* (Paris, 1713), pp. 427–31.
[2] F. M. A. de Voltaire, *Le Cadenas envoyé en 1716 à Madame de B.* (Œuvres complètes (Ed. Garnier), Paris, 1877, vol. ix, pp. 566–8).

Among tne dramatic pieces in which the girdle of chastity plays a part that by Edme Boursault entitled *Les Cadenats* deserves mention. The author, who during his lifetime was not in sympathy with the dramatic work turned out by his greater contemporaries, wrote this piece during the earlier period of his career, and although it is in places both dull and tedious, it exhibits traces of that artistic treatment which can be better discerned in certain of Boursault's more popular works.

The story revolves around a certain governor of Toulon, by name Spadarille, who is jealous of his wife, Olimpie, and has fitted her with six padlocks. Olimpie is beloved by Cléandre, a young man who would have married her had not her father, Alcidor, raised a series of objections. Intrigue between the young people develops; Spadarille becomes more and more suspicious and thinks that " avec mes cadenats, j'ai besoin de verroux ". The outcome of the whole affair is that Olimpie is finally won by Cléandre and the jealous Spadarille is discomforted in spite of all the precautions that he has taken.[1]

Just as in satire and drama the girdle of chastity played its part, so in romance[2] and memoir the device was used to amuse the

[1] E. Boursault, *Théâtre*, Nouvelle éd. (3 vols., Paris, 1725), vol. i, pp. 51–86.
[2] Cf. Pitigrilli [i.e. Dino Segre], *La Cintura di castità* (Milano, 1922).

reader and emphasise the inherent faithlessness
of women and belief in the truth of what Baffo
expressed when he wrote

El gran lucchetto hà d'esser l'onestae.
Quando che'l senso no gà più misura,
La slarga, ve lo zuro, ogni lucchetto,
A costo de sbregar la serradura.[1]

Again in the memoirs of Comte Claude Alexan-
dre de Bonneval occurs a story which has been
quoted as affording evidence of the apocryphal
nature of these documents.[2] Indeed it seems very
doubtful if the work is by Bonneval, and the
authorities at the Bibliothèque Nationale in
Paris ascribe the work to an unknown author.
However that may be, it contains a tale of a
husband who was as jealous as a tiger. The
narrator says that he became enamoured of the
wife of this monster and was amazed to learn
that rumour asserted that he always carried
with him the key of a certain padlock which he
had attached to his wife. At last the possibility
of confirming or denying the rumour occurred
and he hastened to verify it or prove its falsity.
It proved to be well founded. The girdle in this
case was a kind of metallic corset "faite à peu

---

[1] G. Baffo, *op. cit.*, vol. ii, p. 45.
[2] Cf. C. J. de Ligne, *Mémoire sur le Comte de Bonneval*. Nouvelle
éd. (Paris, 1817), p. 5.

près comme le fond d'une fronde " and which made " la route impénetrable ". This grille was attached by chains to a hip belt and it was neither possible to sever nor undo them without detection. Finally the story tells how in Milan it was found possible to have a duplicate key made with the happiest results.[1]

A rather similar adventure was experienced by von Elbenstein which is recorded in that excessively tedious book *Der im Irr-Garten der Liebe herum taumelnde Cavalier* by E. von H., which initials are supposed to refer to Gisander or in other words to J. G. Schnabel. We have here the story of the jealousy of one Oegneck who had prudently his " Lust-Garten mit dem gewöhnlichen Italiänischen Schlosse dergestallt vest verwahrt, dass niemand einsteigen konte ". However, like Cléandre, the lover succeeds in approaching the barrier, and, a wax impression having been made, a duplicate key is soon forthcoming.[2]

In modern times, especially in France, the girdle of chastity still finds a place in the drama and the short story, although it is not profitable

---

[1] [C. A. de Bonneval], *Mémoires du Comte de Bonneval* (2 vols., Londres, 1737), vol. i, pp. 74 ff.

[2] E. von H., *Der im Irr-Garten der Liebe herum taumelnde Cavalier* . . . *Ehedem zusammen getragen durch den Herrn E. v. H.* (2 pts., Warnung-stadt, 1738), p. 351. Paul Ernst, in the 1907 edition of this work, attributes it to J. G. Schnabel, as also does Paul Englisch in his *Geschichte der erotischen Literatur* (Stuttgart, 1926–7), p. 182.

to summarize these works here.[1] Wherever the problem of sexual jealousy is considered there will be found those who will refer to or at least mention that old-established custom of the chastity belt which for so long was thought to be a sure preventive against cuckoldom. There can be no doubt that the majority of husbands had an intense dread of the horns which their faithless wives affixed to their heads, and of illegitimate offspring. They were not all like the husband in the old engraving of the contented cuckold of which there is a copy in the Bibliothèque Nationale in Paris (Tf. 2, 102).

A horned husband is seen emerging from a house carrying a cornucopia. To the left a lover is holding up a bag of money to the wife who shows herself at an upper window with her breasts being fondled by a man in the background. To the right another man enters the house saying that he can lodge better and more comfortably here than in the houses of Venus, since on the house is a notice indicating that rooms are to be had. The husband as he leaves the house gives vent to the following reflections :—

---

[1] Cf. E. Blum and R. Toche, *Le Cadenas* (Paris, 1890), and the stories by such authors as Aurélien Scholl, Louis Lévesque, F. Champsaur and Louis Latourrette mentioned by Caufeynon (*op. cit.*, p. 119), etc.

LITERATURE

De l'encornaillement jamais ie ne Moffence
Au lieu que certains folz s'en mettent au
   desespoir.
Ne m'enquestant de rien et ne uollant rien
   uoir
Pourueu que ce mestier m'aquere labondance.

To such a one a girdle of chastity would have
been no benefit !

CHAPTER VI

IN the preceding chapters we have made a brief survey of the history and use of the girdle of chastity as it is seen in the course of about five hundred years. From the discussion of the evidence it would seem that there is at least the possibility of the idea of the girdle of chastity being derived from that of the infibulation of females, a custom the origin of which is to be sought in the East. Moreover we saw that the Crusaders returning from the Orient may have brought back the idea with them, and that the state of European culture was not one where such a device would have been rejected.

In the course of the argument we remarked that perhaps the earliest representation of a girdle of chastity was that contained in the MS. by Konrad Kyeser called the " Bellifortis ", and that this was a complicated piece of apparatus compared with the specimens which followed it. Generally speaking then we saw that there were seven types of girdles, namely :

(1) The heavy and substantial type represented in the " Bellifortis " (see Plate II, p. 49).

(2) The simple "one piece" girdle of which the specimen (No. 6598) in the Cluny Museum in Paris is a good example (see Pl. VII, p. 96).

(3) The "two piece" girdle with protection both in front and behind which again can be sub-divided into two classes, (a) the simple form, as in the so-called "Carrara" Girdle and the Stockholm Girdle (see Plates III, and VIII), and (b) the handsome and decorated variety of which good examples are No. 6599 in the Cluny Museum (see Plate VII, a, p. 96) and the specimen in the Erbach Castle (see Plate VIII and p. 76).

(4) A simple form of grille apparatus, affording anterior protection only, and supported by chains from a hip band like that described by Chorier (see p. 142).

(5) A broad band of material encircling the loins and thighs to which is attached a band, furnished with the necessary openings and passing between the legs. This is the type which apparently was used both in the Falster Case (see p. 93) and the Rome Case (see p. 113).

(6) A similar piece of apparatus to No. 5 above but made of chain mail and having an opening surrounded with points rather like those which encircle the orifices in the

" Carrara " Girdle. This type is recorded as having been used by Sieur Berhle on Mlle Lajon (see p. 96).

(7) The type devised by John Moodie (see p. 127), where bone or ivory bars are let into a soft cushion or pad, which variety resembles No. 4 above, only that in the former case the grille is attached by belts to tight-fitting drawers instead of being supported by chains to a hip band.

In the majority of girdles adjustment is provided on the hip band and the whole is made secure by some form of locking device attached to the band either at the side, at the back, or in front.

If we admit that Marie de France was referring in her Guigemar Epic to the girdle of chastity, then the date of the introduction of this device into Europe cannot be assigned to a period later than the twelfth century, and even if the evidence furnished by these passages and the corresponding lines of Machaut be rejected, then the appearance of the invention in Italy can be put with certainty in the later years of the fourteenth century or, at the latest, the early years of the fifteenth. Moreover we saw that Italian culture was one which would readily have absorbed the idea of the forcible

restraint of the married woman, and it was noted
how, as the years went by, the use of the girdle
spread to other parts of Europe. The reports
of Brantôme, Buvat, or Tallemant Des Réaux
indicated the widespread application of the
chastity belt among different strata of society,
and the discovery by Pachinger of a female
skeleton with a girdle of chastity in position
suggested strongly that the reports of his
predecessors were not merely idle and baseless
rumours. Finally we saw how the use of the
chastity belt in modern times has led to
proceedings in the courts of law, and how the
device was still being suggested in Great Britain
as a valuable remedy against masturbation
and seduction as late as the middle of the
nineteenth century.

Hence it can be concluded that the girdle
of chastity is a device which has been used
in the past and may be still used to-day;
that it consists of varied forms and diverse
types, and that its object is the same wherever
it is employed, namely the external control
of the *pudendum muliebre* and adjacent regions
for the prevention of illicit intercourse and
auto-erotic satisfaction, and also for preventing
illegitimate children. The device thus falls into
line with those other mechanical methods for
enforcing continence which are known in various

parts of the world. As a monument of human folly the girdle of chastity is a good example : as an indication of the lengths to which jealousy unchecked will lead it is unique. There can be little doubt that the imposition of chastity belts upon women in order to allay masculine jealousy, and the operation of infibulation upon male slaves by their mistresses for the sake of lust, are two of the most remarkable customs ever devised by mankind in its efforts to control the intricacies of the erotic life.

INDEX OF AUTHORITIES QUOTED

Alembert, 99
Amour (L') en fureur, 144 ff.
Areco, 11
Aretino, 27, 131, 150
Audeber, 31

Baffo, 6, 22, 25, 27, 156
Bannatyne, 133, 136
Baretti, 31
Bartels, 79
Barthélemy, 49
Bartsch, 71
Bauer, B., 18
Bauer, M., 24, 61
Beaumanoir, 24
Berchet, 36, 43
Berliner Tageblatt, 122
Béroalde de Verville, 59
Beutler, 132
Bibra, 61
Bilder-Lexikon der Erotik, 122, 132
Billon, 29, 37
Block, 122
Blum, 158
Boissieu, 72
Bonneau, 44, 50, 97
Bonneval, 156
Bordier, 10
Borrow, 11
Boudyck-Bastiaanse, 13
Boursault, 155
Bouvignes, 30
Brant, 51, 52, 69
Brantôme, 45 ff., 105, 163
Broca, 32
Bromley, 40
Brosses, 41, 43
Brunet, 151
Burnat-Provins, 24
Busnelli, 9
Buvat, 50, 163

Cabanès, 98
Cambridge Modern History, 35
Campardon, 50
Camus, 98
Carré, 106
Casanova, 101
Caufeynon, 9, 18, 106, 113
Cazanova, 101, 103
Cecchetti, 25
Celsus, 110
Champsaur, 158
Charpentier, 150
Chorier, 60, 140 ff., 161
Colbert, 39
Collyer, 109
Cornazzano, 144
Coryat, 37
Coulton, 7

D***, 151
Daily (The) Telegraph, 115
Daniëls, 67, 81
Davenport, 43
Debay, 106, 108
Delicado, 24
Desessarts, 99
Deutscher Reichsanzeiger, 122
Diderot, 99
Dilling, 11
Dingwall, 2, 4, 55, 110
Dufay, 150
Dufour, 18, 44
Dulaure, 43

Einckel, 40
Englisch, 157
Ernst, 157
Ersch, 42, 106
Eschbach, 56
Escole (L') des Filles, 149, 150
Estienne, 30
Evelyn, 37
Evening Star, 59

F***, M., 99
Facetiae facetiarum, 139
Fauconney, 9
Feldhaus, 6, 34, 62, 82
Fiedler, 11
Fischart, 54
Fleury, 43
France (La) Littéraire, 99
Franckius, 3
Frauenzimmerschule (Die), 60, 61
Freksa, 132
Freydier, 95, 97 ff.
Fuchs, 2, 18, 62, 64, 65, 68, 70,
    73, 74, 79, 121, 132

Gaultier, 49
Geisberg, 62
Gironde (La), 113
Gisander, 157
Goncourt, E. and J. de, 6
Gould, 109
Grapow, 9
Gregory, *of Tours*, 111
Gruber, 42, 106
Grupp, 19
Guerrini, 27
Gui, *de Bourgoyne*, 24
Gynäologie, 55

H., E. von, 157
Hagen, 23
Helot, 150
Hémard, 108
Hennisart, 151
*Heureuses (Les) advantures
    d'amour*, 137
Hirschfeld, 150
Huguetan, 38, 39

*Inventaire-Sommaire . . . de
    Nîmes*, 98

Jablonsky, 41
Jalado-Lafond, 122, 126
Journal (Le), 115
Jousseaume, 12
Jung, 79

Kahn, 115
Kallianwalla, 110

Kemmerich, 115
Kind, 70
Kirchner, 80
Krämer, 13
Krauss, 13
Krünitz, 6, 41, 55
Kyeser, 33 ff., 90, 160

L., Ch., 98
Laborde, 17, 18
Lacroix, 18
La Fontaine, 13
Lassels, 31, 38
Legati, 4
Legros, 110
Lévesque, 158
Liberal (El), 106
Ligne, 156
Litta, 42
Liverdys, 38
Loubier, 24
Lyndsay, 133 ff.

M., E., 9, 50
Machaut, 16, 17, 89, 162
Maier, 42
Mantegazza, 18
Marconville, 29
Marcotti, 27
Mareuil, 20
Marie, *de France*, 14, 15, 89, 162
Marot, 22, 132
Maupassant, 105
Maynard, 108
Ménard, 98
Méschanceté (La) des Filles, 57 ff.
Métivet, 116
Meursius, 141
Mililot, 150
Milot, 150
Mirabal, 40
Misson, 39, 40
Moll, 122, 149
Molmenti, 25, 26
Montaiglon, 30
Montesquieu, 105
Moodie, 61, 123 ff., 162
Morlini, 129, 131
Moyen (Le) de Parvenir, 58 ff.

INDEX OF AUTHORITIES QUOTED

Müller, 55
Musset, 105

Nanteuil, 137
Nebbio, 36
Neickelius, 40
Neumann, 62
News (The) of the World, 115
Nicolas, 97
Niel, 66
Nisard, 151
Noury, 6, 111

Pachinger, 80, 81, 84 ff., 90, 163
Pallas, 12
Patin, 150
Pauw, 6
People (The), 115
Petermann, 150
Petit (Le) Parisien, 115
Pitigrilli, 155
Ploss, 79
Poggio, 2, 27
Power, 7
Prutz, 18, 19
Pyle, 109

Rabelais, 54, 133
Reitzenstein, 79
Renier, 21 ff.
Riolanus, 3
Rire (Le), 116
Ritter, 37
Rizat, 110
Rodocanachi, 26, 28
Roger Bontemps en belle humeur, 137, 140
Roquelaure, 140

Saint-Amant, 136
Saint-Didier, 26
Savoie-Carignan, 49
Scherr, 61
Schidlof, 13
Schidrowitz, 103, 148

Schmid, 76
Schmidt, 65
Schnabel, 157
Scholl, 158
Schrenck, 12
Schultz, 15, 24, 34, 61
Schurig, 3
Segre, 155
Semerau, 24
Sercambi, 26
Sharp, 31, 32
Sigæa, 140, 141, 144
Simson, 11
Sir, 108
Soloviev, 110
Sommerard, 82
Spon, 150
Stern, 12

Tallemant Des Réaux, 47, 48, 163
Tannhauser, 24
Temps (Le), 113
Thompson, 74
Tlusty, 108
Toche, 158
Tola-Paix, 10
Touchet, 148

Valentini, 94
Veryard, 40
Voigt, 22
Voltaire, 105, 154

Wall, 18
Will, 65
Williams, 50
Witkowski, 32
Worm, 93, 94
Wulff, 30

X . . ., 12

Zanotto, 42
*Zeichen und Wert d. verletzen
. . . Jungfrauschaft*, 55
Zwingäuer, 23

INDEX OF SUBJECTS

Adam, Baffo's compassion for, 22; portrayed on Cluny Museum girdle, 82

Africa, origin of girdle of chastity in, 10; female infibulation in, 12

Ago plant, 13

Agnes, *of Navarre*, 17

Albi, 72

Alcidor, 155

Aldegrever, 70

Alessio, 146, 147

Amman, 65

America, girls of, 60; infibulation of females in, 109

Amsterdam, 81

Ancilotti, 113

Anne, *of Austria*, 50

Arles, 137

Armoury, the small in Venice, 36 ff.

Arsenal Museum, Venice, 36

Auto-erotism, in Italy, 26. *See also* Masturbation

B., Anna, 111 ff.

Baldung (Grün), 62

Barbers, Venetian, 27, 59

Barcelona, 71

Baths, Venetian, 27

Baudouin, 105

Beatrice, 21

Beaucaire, 96

Beauty, cult of, 20; of female body, 21 ff.; of male body, 24

Bellifortis, 33

Benevente, 106

Bergamo, 133

Berlhe, 95, 96, 162

Bessy, 134 ff.

Body, beauty of female, 21 ff.; beauty of male, 24; as source of pleasure, 25

Bohemia, 108

Bolivia, 13

Bolzano, 80

Bonn, Andreas, 81

Bordeaux, 111 ff.

Boucher, 105

Branding, of parents, 25

Breasts, beauty of female, 21 ff.; exposed, 30, 37

Brest, 72

Buonavista, 106

Byzantium, 19

Cambon, 117 ff.

Camille, 148

Carrara, Alexius, 41 ff.

Carrara, Francesco, 35 ff., 90, 161; jealousy of, 42

Cassagnes-Comtaux, 117, 119

Catherine, *de Medici*, 50

Causes Grasses, 97, 98

Celebes, North, 13, 14

Chastity, Girdle of, *see* Girdle of Chastity

Chastity, of gypsies in Spain, 11

Cicisbeism, 31 ff.

Circassia, 11

Cléandre, 155

Cluny Museum, girdles of chastity in, 82 ff.; 161

Condom, early form of, 150

Conversion, of prostitutes, 28

Corn-cutters, 27

Courts, of Love, 57

Croats, 13

Crusades, 18, 89, 160

Denmark, 93

Dress, immodest, of French girls, 30; of Venetian women, 37

Elbenstein, 157

Eleonora di Sciampagna, 51

INDEX OF SUBJECTS

Elizabeth Farnese, *of Parma*, 72
" Enfer " section, at Bibliothèque Nationale, 102
Entail, 125
Erbach, 76 ; girdles of chastity at, 76 ff., 161
Esqúetor, 26
Eve, portrayed on Cluny Museum girdle, 82
Eyes, beauty of, 21

Fabricius, 145 ff.
Falster, 93, 100, 161
Flötner, 62
Flogging, of parents, 25
Freidier, A., 98
Fürst, 70
Fyffe, 135

Gaultier, 66
Gaumier, 114
Genoa, 19
Girdle of Chastity, nomenclature of, 4 ; types of, 5, 160 ff. ; for males, 6, 151 ; dating of, 7 ; origin of, 10, 18, 35, 41, 160 ; introduction into Europe, 33, 160 ; of Carrara, 35 ff., 161, 162 ; introduction into Italy, 44, 162 ; introduction into France, 44 ; of Mlle de Valois, 49 ff. ; in Germany, 51 ff. ; of Müller, 55 ff. ; in Peruvian nunneries, 61 ; photographs of, 71 ; estimated number of, 71 ; in French museums, 72 ; in Madrid, 72 ; in Witt Collection, 73 ; in Wellcome Historical Medical Museum, 74 ; in Royal College of Surgeons, 74 ; in Madame Tussaud's, 74 ; in Munich, 74 ; at Erbach, 76, 161 ; in Kalmar, 76 ; at Castle Runkelstein, 80 ff. ; in Amsterdam, 81 ; in Vienna, Berlin, Würzburg and Paris, 82 ; discovered on skeleton, 84 ff., 90, 163 ; and the law, 92 ff. ; case at Falster of, 93 ff., 100,

161 ; case at Nîmes of, 95 ff., 162 ; Cazanova-Carré case concerning, 101 ff. ; Spanish case of, 106 ; Weimar case of, 106 ; French case of, 107 ; Bordeaux case of, 111 ff. ; Rome case of, 113 ff. ; Parat case of, 115 ff. ; prospectuses of, 117 ff. ; patent for, 122 ; modern inquiries for, 123 ; Moodie's account of, 124 ff. ; in literature, 129 ff. ; said to be mentioned by Marot, 132 ff.
Girdles, virgin, of antiquity, 10
Girls, dress of French, 30 ; morals of eighteenth century, 57 ; morality of mining, 125
Godemiché, 126, 128
Göttingen, 34
Golziera, 35
Goubert, 151 ff.
Greuze, 105
Guigemar Epic, 14, 162

Henri II, 50
Henri IV, 66
Homosexuality, in Italy, 26
Hôtel de Rambouillet, 48
Hufferte, 111 ff.

Impressions, pre-natal, 147
Infanticide, 54
Infibulation, male, 2, 164
Infibulation, female, 3, 32, 89, 160 ; in Africa, 12 ; in Bohemia, 108 ff. ; in America, 109 ; in Leicester, 110 ; in India, 110 ; in France, 110
Ismaël, 147
Italy, jealousy in, 25, 28, 37, 138 ; infidelity of women in, 31 ; kissing in, 31

Jay, 48
Jealousy, Italian, 25, 28, 37, 138 ; Hémard on, 108
Jerusalem, 102
Jocondo, 141
Julia, 141

Kalmar, 76
Kissing, in Italy, 31

Lajon, 95, 162
Lambeye, 111 ff.
Laura, 21
Law, the girdle of chastity and the, 92 ff.
Legend, the Carrara, 35 ff., 90
Leicester, 110
León, 106
Lesbian love, in the Nogarola family, 26
Leyden, 66, 81
Literature, of cuckoldom, 1; erotic, 8, 20; anti-feminist, 29; the girdle of chastity and, 129 ff.
Lombardy, 133
Louis XIII, 50
Luchetto, 36

Madrid, 72
Maria Louisa, *of Savoy*, 72
Maroto, 106
Masturbation, 55; devices to prevent, 56, 121 ff.; results of, 125. *See also* Auto-erotism
Maulschloss, 54
Mérimée, 83
Merkin, 150
Middle Ages, sexual life in the, 20
Milan, 131, 157
Minnesingers, 23
Misses, Boarding-School, 125
Modena, the Prince of, 49
Monasteries, vice in, 27
Montpellier, 95, 97, 99
Montauban, 72
Munich, 74
Museo Storico Navale, 36

Nîmes, 95 ff.; Presidial Court at, 98 ff.
Nogarola, family of, 26
Norcia, statues, 28
Nunneries, vice in, 26, 27; Peruvian, 61

Octavia, 141
Oddone de Faix, 51
Oegneck, 157
Offspring, illegitimate, 158, 163
Olimpie, 155
Othello, 115

Padua, 35
Parat, 115 ff.
Passalina, 114
Patent, for girdle of chastity, 122
Perrone d'Armentières, 17
Philip V, 72
Pieroni, 115
Pisa, 18
Pledge, of fidelity, 15
Poitiers, 72; girdle in Museum at, 73
Poland, 12
Pope, the, and Italian children, 60
Population, problem of, 47
Prospectuses, of girdles of chastity, 117 ff.
Prostitutes, customs of Italian, 27; freedom of in Italy, 28, 89; conversion of eighty-two, 28
Prostitution, of children, 25; in Venice, 26, 27, 37
Provence, 137
Punishment, for sexual offences in Italy, 25 ff.

Quimper, 72

Randone, 113
Renaissance, 20 ff., 129
Rennes, 72
Rignac, 117
Rome, 27, 113, 161
Roujan, 102, 103
Royal College of Surgeons, 74
Runkelstein, castle, 80; girdle found at, 80 ff.

Sainct-Germain, 45
Saint-Gilles, 96
Samoa, 13
Samoyedes, jealousy of the, 12

INDEX OF SUBJECTS

Schäfer, 122
Schedel, bookplate of, 65
Seduction, method to avoid, 127
Scotland, 133
Sempronia, 142, 143
Sens, 72
Sjaellamd, 93
Sodomy, in Asia, 19 ; in Arabian culture, 19 ; in England, 19 ; among Frankish peoples, 19 ; in Italy, 19, 27
Spadarille, 155
Spain, 106 ; gypsies in, 11
Stiévenin, 112
Stockholm, 161
Sudan, female infibulation in the, 12

Tonnochy, 73
Toulon, 155
Transvestitism, 27
Troubadours, 20
Tullia, 141
Tussaud's, Madame, 74

Urine, virtue of female, 29

Vallet Collection, 97
Valois, Mlle de, 49
Vannes, 72
Venice, a centre of Oriental trade, 18 ; prostitution in, 26, 27, 37 ; baths of, 27 ; barbers of, 27, 59 ; wickedness of, 26, 31
Verneuil, the Marquise de, 66
Virginie, 145 ff.
Virginity, tests for, 59
Vogtherr, 62, 65

Watteau, 105
Weimar, 106
Wine, the Milk of Venus, 59
Wellcome Historical Medical Museum, 74
Witt, George, Collection of, 73
Women, aspersions on, 29 ; in Italy, 25, 29, 37 ; urine of, 29 ; as animals, 30 ; as half saints, half devils, 89 ; morality of Scottish, 126 ff.
Wormus, 101 ff.

York, the Duke of, 6

Zamora, 106

171